THE LIFE AND WORKS OF BESSIE HEAD

Virginia Uzoma Ola

The Edwin Mellen Press
Lewiston/Queenston/Lampeter

Library of Congress Cataloging-in-Publication Data

Ola, Virginia Uzoma.
   The life and works of Bessie Head / Virginia Uzoma Ola.
      p.   cm.
   Includes bibliographical references (p.) and index.
   ISBN 0-7734-9018-3
   1. Head, Bessie, 1937-   . 2. Women and literature--South Africa-
-History--20th century. 3. Women authors, South African--20th
century--Biography.   I. Title.
PR9369.3.H4Z82   1994
823--dc20
   [B]   94-20128
                                                                 CIP

A CIP catalog record for this book is available from the British Library.

Copyright © 1994 The Edwin Mellen Press

   The Edwin Mellen Press   The Edwin Mellen Press
           Box 450   Box 67
     Lewiston, New York   Queenston, Ontario
     USA 14092-0450   CANADA L0S 1L0

                    The Edwin Mellen Press, Ltd.
                       Lampeter, Dyfed, Wales
                    UNITED KINGDOM SA48 7DY

             Printed in the United States of America

For my husband and best friend, Akinlabi;
my children; Ayo, Dipo, Tunde and Ebele.
Like an ever-flowing stream they always sustain.

TABLE OF CONTENTS

PREFACE

Interest in a topic or an author can originate in different ways. Some critics can easily pinpoint a moment, a place or a person on whom the initial impulse can be located; the one who dropped the first idea or uttered the particular sentence, consciously or unconsciously. For other critics however it is more difficult to say exactly when their interest in an author began. Inspite of that several readers remember reading a book for the first time, re-reading it and slowly finding it grow on them. That was my experience with the works of Bessie Head. I cannot remember the first time Maru fell into my hands, but I do recollect vividly going back to it several times and ultimately searching out the other works by Bessie Head. Soon the ideas and feelings that bind all the works together began to emerge: the uncanny combination of sensitivity and strength that runs through them. Character types also began to emerge all typified by clashing personality traits. I could also see that there was space in the landscape for both men and women, young and old, natives and visitors, the weak and the strong the oppressor and the oppressed. What was most interesting about this mode of writing was that it fell into a trilogy and finally spread its tentacles to other literary types like the short story, the historical and ethnographic modes.

I tested my growing admiration for Head's talent by including Maru in my African Novel course in the University of Benin, Nigeria from 1985 to 1987. Before then Bessie Head had participated in our International African Literature Conference at the University of Calabar in 1982 and had rattled most of us emotionally with her horrifying personal life-history of chilling loneliness and racial isolation and her obsessive search for roots and personal identity which grew from that experience.

Listening to Head deliver her paper served as a catalyst which convinced me that the author was positing a very original and personal ideology which sought to link literature, this time, African literature to its age-old functions of entertaining and teaching at the same time. Head believed so deeply in the ability of literature to do this that she did not mind submerging her whole life experience into it and using her personal and political experience in Botswana and South Africa as the raw materials with which to delve into what she considered the mysteries and magic of human life, and to examine that inscrutable presence of the good and bad in every individual, with the ultimate intention of presenting mankind with the near-ideal society.

In discussions of Bessie Head's works with African academics in the early nineteen eighties I observed a type of general and tragic impatience with her themes and style much like what happened to Ayi Kwei Armah's reputation after his publication of <u>The Beautyful Ones are not yet Born.</u> Several African critics claimed she was too autobiographical; Lewis Nkosi is one of such critics. Others complained she was too utopian and the final group thought <u>A Question of Power</u> was too complex stylistically to make much sense or be taken seriously. This reaction is proved by the fact that till today most critics of her novels are non-African, although since her death in April 1986 her reputation among African academics has grown steadily. The tragedy of her death also compelled me to embark on putting into a book form some articles I had written on her and to explore further what I considered the total achievement of such a humane writer who was able to transcend her personal abuses as a women, an orphan and an outsider in her society to extol all that is positive in human relationships and criticise all that is evil, even in African traditional practices. The major themes of her imaginative enterprise grew more complex from text to text.

Stylistically it is difficult not to be captivated by the sheer poetry of her utterances in any discourse she adopted. In a literary universe broken up into ideological and stylistic camps she was able to bring all forms of injustices, starting with the Apartheid system in South Africa, including sexism and racism under a humanistic umbrella where human beings became the criteria for measuring the worth of any system of human association. Her creative writings were her only weapons for bridging the gaps and for breaking the barriers against an integrated pluralistic discourse where the utopian, feminist and humanist meet. That is why her talent has defied categorisation.

She fought ugliness with the beauty of language and exposed to her readers the beauty in every human soul and in the universe at large.

It is only fitting that nearly ten years after her death her tributes should continue to grow with one more devoted to highlighting the intractable nature of her quiet but tough genius.

ACKNOWLEDGEMENTS

"Women in Bessie Head's Ideal World" first appeared in <u>ARIEL - A Review of International English Literature</u> Calgary, Canada. 1986 . "The Question of Good and Evil in Head's Ideal World" first appeared as a chapter in <u>The Tragic Life</u> - Bessie Head and Literature in South Africa. (ed) Cecil Abrahams and published by Africa World Press, Trenton N. J. 1990 I am grateful for the privilege to use these articles.

I also most sincerely express my gratitude to Professor Cecil Abrahams for his friendship and encouragement of my interest in Bessie Head. My thanks also go to Mr. Toyin Adepoju of the Department of English and Literature, University of Benin, Nigeria for bringing me several useful articles on Bessie Head from different sources.

CHAPTER ONE

In an age of explosion and such proliferation of literary theories, each placing emphasis upon one function rather than another, it seems almost quaint, ultra conservative, even recalcitrant to base the assessment of a body of literary works on the now almost forgotten and-no-longer-so-fashionable romantic approach which considers the writer's mind and life of vital importance; and also the phenomenological approach which emphasises the reader's response to the work and its message, in the "ancient" Leavis mode. Postcolonial discourse cannot at this political and historical moment run away from these approaches, because to do so would be to deny its essence, since one of its most noticeable attributes is a self-conscious posture which quite often automatically presupposes a statement, direct or implied. It contradicts Formalism and its text-centred approach in preference to a mode where matters of reference, social, historical, racial, sexual continue to insist on their essentiality; in other words a context in which the traditional methods of socio-historical scholarship continue to have validity, while respecting the relevance of language and language structure. It is still willing to let the text speak to its readers on matters of human life, those lofty ideas propounded by Leavis. The postcolonial creative writer often gives the impression of writing out of compulsion; cultural, historical and political; to communicate a message. In some cases the meaning is more important than the process of decoding and deconstructing the text. Criticism should not shy away from extricating that meaning from a mire of intellectual and critical postures which threaten to sacrifice it to the act of its own creation and deny its validity, centrality and authenticity. It must also resist a philosophical position which challenges it to accept that since truth has become so fragmented, cynicism is a more sensible alternative to optimism.

Postcolonial literature is still deeply involved in the process of re-writing texts and in this task, social and historical imperatives must be allowed to exist side by side with the more text-based formalist approach which is satisfied, and almost celebrates its ability to ignore the impact of a work of art on its reader. Writers write from a multitude of complex reasons, such as, in many black writers, the reality of hundreds of years of overt and covert enslavement, exploitation and degradation of black people, which Henry Louis Gates Jr. explores in The Signifying Monkey: A Theory of Afro-American Literary Criticism (1988). Brad Bucknell (1990) describes this work as the author's attempt to find a distinctively black method of reconciling history and form, textuality and experience, at least in part through a reappropriation of contemporary critical theory.[1] The fact that some Afro-American critics disagree with Gates reinforces the necessity for a sensitive discrimination based on an understanding and acknowledgement of such historical and cultural realities.

In the case of African Literature the necessity for such specificity becomes more urgent, since analogy has often tended to blur the fine lines and differences not only racially but also creatively; that is in the author's conception of what his or her role is. At the 1990 MLA Convention held in Chicago, Susan Lanser in a powerful paper insists that the basis for naming in such instances should be specificity not sameness or difference because everyone is alone; is an island harbouring painful experiences in different forms (Chicago, 1990).[2]

With reference to African Literature, much of the large corpus of critical material which followed the publication of the first set of indigenous writings remained submerged in a circular controversy over the questions of definition, evaluative criteria and language. Central to the debate was the necessity to

---

[1] Brad Bucknell, "Henry Louis Gates, Jr. and the Theory of Signifying" ARIEL - a Review of International English Literature 21:1, 1990

[2] Susan Lanser, "The Edges that Blur: Women's Studies, Cultural Studies and the Politics of Analogy". Chicago: MLA Convention, 1990.

safeguard it from becoming a new tradition perpetually tagging along the dominant and longer established Western counterpart. The issue was one of evolving a separate and incontestable identity which critical canon must acknowledge. In reverse therefore, the creative writer was also expected to be committed to a set of recognisable themes, experiences and forms which would contribute to the emergence of the tradition as a special entity.

The argument over commitment perhaps will remain unresolved for a long time because of its ideological and nationalistic overtones. Many African critics still feel indisposed to accept as committed, works which criticise the shortcomings of their societies, especially Ayi Kwei Armah's The Beautiful Ones are not yet Born (Heinemann, 1968)[3] with its forthright attack on corruption, greed and nepotism. As a summary statement on the controversy, Eustace Palmer writes:

> In sum then, I am suggesting that the criticism of African fiction should take into account both the relevance of the work to the human condition (the sociological, if one prefers the term, and the novelist's artistry. And artistry should include coherence of plot, and structure, language (making suitable allowances for any necessity and deliberate modifications the writer may have made in order to accommodate his insights, setting, presentation of character, descriptive power and so on.[4]

The South African writer, because of his peculiar social and political circumstances, suffered more from this pressure with the result that occasionally he sacrificed true art to ideological pronouncements. The urge to recreate personal experiences in fiction naturally predisposed him towards the autobiographical. Often protest and commitment became synonymous in such works. The political, social and emotional loomed so large in the landscape that authors needed very mature artistry to keep their works from degenerating into crude propaganda.

Bessie Head stands apart for her ability to transcend that weakness. But

---

[3] Ayi Kwei Armah: The Beautyful Ones are not yet Born. London, Ibadan: Heinemann, 1968

[4] Eustace Palmer, The Growth of the African Novel. London, Ibadan, Nairobi: Heinemann, 1979, p.9.

Head ironically has been criticised for not demonstrating clear interest in politics. Lewis Nkosi charges:

> Bessie Head is not a political novelist in any sense we can recognise; indeed there is ample evidence that she is generally hostile to politics. Far from being an axiomatic proposition, as some critics with an innate hostility to politics tend to believe; this lack of precise political commitment weakens rather than aids Bessie Head's grasp of character.[5]

Nkosi's one-sided critical perception errs on the side of balance in equating creative failure with a lack of recognizable political posture. What he perceives as Head's weakness, characterisation; is admired by other critics as an obvious strength. Although Head places her writing in the context of her own struggle against discrimination in South Africa and Botswana, she musters enough creative objectivity to give her readers a variety of characters, male and female, facing their individual turmoil in different ways, and with varying degrees of success. But their totality as human beings transcends politics, and is fully realised in spite of it. Her works have a distinctive Bessie Head's voice which speaks through history, politics, legend, myth, fantasy and psychology, but refuses to sacrifice optimism to dry cynicism. She functions from what she calls "the dead calm centre of a storm that rages over the whole of Southern Africa". Despite this recognition she always searches out for what she considers as Botswana's quiet strengths. Her commitment celebrates those strengths while exposing the weaknesses. She once described her own style as "concise and taut" not "loose and baggy". With such a subtle and personalised style the advocates of political commitment in literature find her less than successful in character portrayal. The irony of Head's position is indeed that her mature literary vision is a true assault on the shortcomings of such extremist theories of literature.

Although committed literature forms the bulk of African Literature, its usual and facile identification with Socialist, Marxist or simply anti-colonial discourse has tended to narrow the scope of its possibilities, and to exclude from

---

[5] Lewis Nkosi. Tasks and Masks, Themes and Styles of African Literature. United Kingdom: Longman, 1981, p. 102.

its fold bodies of literature which rightly belong there. It also ignores the subtle permutations which such literary vision can assume. In such a limited context also, commitment soon becomes populist and culturist, and any writer or work which falls short of its prescriptions is soon dismissed as reactionary in its vision. This crude and insensitive partitioning which fails to recognise the subtle play of delicate social and emotional forces in human lives also fails to appreciate that literature works by indirection.

African Literature has just begun to scratch at the surface of the social pressures and practices which direct our decisions and relationships with one another. It is still to go beyond the wounds of colonialism to explore the internal weaknesses within our traditions that often hold the human spirit in bondage and explain human actions. It is still to confront the larger abstract issues of love, justice and power. In other words literature is, and will for some time continue to be a social practice directed towards the foundations of a viable human order in our societies. This is an expansive philosophy already experimented upon by Bessie Head. Politics, love, religion clash in human motivations in a progressive manner which subtly insists that in spite of pain, failure, disappointment, all must work for a better tomorrow for all. Those who look for large ideological statements are often disappointed because they fail to recognise a more fundamental approach which shows that man is a political animal, and whether he likes it or not he lives politics daily, since his life is inevitably influenced by the political decisions of those in power, be they traditional chiefs, the elders in the society, colonial rulers or their representatives. This understanding underlies Head's examination of the realities of power and oppression in all forms: personal, economic, sexual, religious and of course political. She saw it as her duty to help correct what is wrong and highlight what is right, for emulation.

Bessie Head's work is therefore subtly didactic and overtly functional. She defines her approach to creative writing thus:

> ...I would never fall in the category of a writer who produces light entertainment...My whole force and direction come from having something to say. What we are mainly very bothered about has been the dehumanizing of black people. And if we can resolve our difficulties it is because we want a future which is defined for our children. So then we can't sort of say that you

have ended any specified thing or that you have changed the
world. You have merely offered your view of a grander world,
of a world that's much grander than the one we've had already.[6]

These lines tell us why Head wrote; it was an attempt to fulfil what she
saw as her role in building a grander world for black people and everybody
else. The themes she selected, the events she created, the characters she chose
and the landscape they move in are direct aspects and qualities of that world she
never stopped building. She did not create geniuses, or villains, just human
beings, sometimes grand, other times scarred, but all marching relentlessly
towards, and participating in, the realisation of her comprehensive social vision
which evolves naturally from the vicissitudes of our corporate existence. Abiola
Irele once wrote in reference to Nigeria literature:

> It is no exaggeration to say that every work of literature produced
> in this country is in some way or other a testimony to the inner
> realities of the social processes at work among us and to the
> tensions these have set up in our collective consciousness. (Irele,
> 1988)[7]

In a way most literature is about that testimony. Most writers explore
these inner realities; some criticise them, some even praise them, but few ever
go beyond to apply them towards the construction of an alternative social order.
Thoreau once attempted it and left us with Walden. Bessie Head found Serowe,
reconstructed it into a grander world of humane possibilities. She stretched the
functionality of literature to its ultimate. She left us her works and her world.
The following essays have attempted to marry these works to the world she
created through them; their true objective correlative.

Chapter Two explores the operation of the dual principles of good and
evil in human lives and society, and the often conflicting roles of both within
the same personality. In the insecure and oppressive context of South Africa it
assumes a deep psychological form, and undergoes a profound personal

---

[6] Voice of America. Interview with Lee Nichols (1981, 55-56).

[7] Abiola Irele, "Literary Criticism in the Nigerian Context," in Perspectives on Nigerian
Literature, 1700 to the Present. Vol. 1, Wale Ogunyemi, (ed.) Nigeria, Guardian Books
Nigerian Limited, 1988.

interpretation.

Chapter Three analyses Head's attitude towards the roles and deprivations of women in South Africa and Botswana. Her own childhood, upbringing and unimaginable cruelty of some of those she came across form the background of her exploration and beliefs. She is a critic of weak women but a crusader for their rights within and without the family. Her works portray a cross-section of women of different ages and in different economic and psychological situations, and from different parts of the world. Each has a uniqueness which underscores her respect for their essence as human beings with a special role in society.

Head's love of nature is amply demonstrated by her decision to spend her whole life in the little rural and arid community of Botswana with its variety of dry grass, crops, frail stalks and little streams; its dusty footpaths, brooding clouds and eternal sunlight; and the perfect harmony between these phenomena and human lives. Chapter Four is an attempt to explore the meaning of this harmony and spiritual energy to Bessie Head.

Chapter Five analyses the role of the short stories and ethnographic accounts in her last books within her overall creative endeavour, while Chapter Six serves as a tribute to Head and her work; and establishes her position in the tradition of African Literature as an idealist and realist, a feminist and utopian writer, a historian, story-teller and ethnographer, but mostly an insatiable and unshakeable optimist, who never wavered in her belief in the ability of human beings to create a better world than the one they live in.

The final chapter underscores her achievement further by ultimately comparing her with two other African women writers, and in the attempt positing theoretical strategies for the attainment of the desirable thematic and formalistic authenticity, and artistic maturity in which Head has excelled.

CHAPTER TWO

The Question of Good and Evil in Head's Novels

> Maybe a dark shadow had been created to balance the situation.
> Maybe some blot of human wrong had to happen to force Maru
> to identify himself with the many wrongs of mankind.[1]

It is significant that the foregoing lines should appear in a passage which describes a garden of yellow daisies where a lover meditates on the boundless joys of a romantic relationship whose days of "torrential expressions of love" far outweigh the occasional malice and unhappiness which are always part of most human situations.

Maru, the protagonist of Bessie Head's novel, is in love with nature, particularly the yellow daisies which dotted the surroundings of his little house on a hill, mainly because they "were the only flowers which resembled the face of his wife and the sun of his love" (p.5). Despite this fairy-tale and magical environment the love in question is haunted by "a low line of black boiling clouds" which manifests itself in vicious malicious moods occasioned by the guilt of its violation of Margaret's first love which Maru, her husband, had executed without remorse. Maru's victory of necessity is therefore tainted by evil and its agony follows him all the days of his life.

This structure of the conflict of good and evil in human lives and society is central in Bessie Head's vision and controls the structural landscape and

---

[1] Bessie Head, Maru London: Heinemann, 1971, p.8. Further references to this text can be found within the essay.

characterization in her three novels. Invariably it is engendered by the ruthless and unjust exercise of power.

This dichotomy attains its most frightening dimension in A Question of Power from which readers emerge unable to establish any connection between the harrowing experience recorded therein and the beautiful pastoral scenes which straddle those scenes. Behind all these are the nightmarish accounts of intrigue, hatred, callousness and intense mental torture which the main character is subjected to. Commenting on this aspect of her works, Head herself says:

> Such peaceful rural scenes would be hastily snatched to form the backdrop to tortuous novels. Perceptive fans sensed the disparity, the disparity between the peaceful simplicity of village life and a personality more complex than village life could ever be. They would say: "I like the bits about Botswana life but I found your second/third novel difficult to read..."[2]

The above statement defines succinctly the dominant structural design of Head's novels, which she herself has called "tortuous." It was in the attempt to come to grips with that same overpowering quality, especially in A Question of Power, that Arthur Ravenscroft wrote:

> It seems to me that with Bessie Head..each novel both strikes out anew, and also reshoulders the same burden. It is as if one were observing a process that involves simultaneously progression, introgression, and circumgression; but also (and here I believe lies her particular creative power) organic growth in both her art and her central concerns. For all our being lured as readers into the labyrinth of Elizabeth's tortured mind in A Question of Power, and then, as it were, left there to face with her the phantasmagoric riot of nightmare and horror, one nevertheless senses throughout that the imagination which unleashes this fevered torrent resides in a creative mind that is exceedingly tough.[3]

---

[2] Bessie Head, "Biographical Notes: A Search for of Historical Continuity and Roots". A short Paper presented by the author at the Annual International Conference of African Literature held at the University of Calabar, Nigeria, February 1982

[3] Arthur Ravenscroft: "The Novels of Bessie Head" in Aspects of South African Literature (ed.) Christopher Heywood London, Ibadan, Nairobi, Lusaka: Heinemann, 1976, p. 175.

This toughness accounts for the special bleakness which we find in her moral vision and world view, for despite their constant celebration of rural harmony, innocence, love and solidarity; qualities vital for the creation of the "new worlds" which Head advocates ceaselessly in these novels, it also shows that in that moral quest she never loses sight of the harsh realities, such as racism, sexism, poverty and sometimes fear, which threaten the full realization of that dream. The cooperative in <u>When Rain Clouds Gather</u> is such a new world, at least its possibility, which the characters attempt to create from the harsh and dry landscape of rural Botswana, and from the broken pieces of their past. Head's vision is dominated by visionaries, the creators of these new worlds, and the demons which constantly thwart their efforts, through political or sexual power. Head herself has admitted that her earlier work was filled with "personal data and responses to challenges that were on the whole internal, private."[4] The different stages of that life are recreated in her three novels mostly through the experiences of characters whose problems articulate Head's own moral vision and fear of power.

This vision includes a keen search for human, social, sexual and political values within a harmonious social order. Understandably the limitations of women's roles, their disadvantages and their bruised self-image feature prominently in her novels. The black and coloured of South Africa, women and all the politically oppressed, are victims of the power she dreads so much. <u>When Rain Clouds Gather</u>, her first novel, deals with the search for roots from different perspectives, and as it affects characters of different social backgrounds, all victims of political, tribal, sexual or even religious power. The book reminds the reader of the drought-stricken world of Ngugi wa Thiongo's <u>Petals of Blood</u> where characters with different visions and problems bond together in search of political justice and spiritual regeneration. Makhaya is such a character.

He is a typical victim of political power that manifests itself in racial oppression, a situation which Head knows by personal experience. As a young Zulu, he fled into Botswana like Head herself, to escape prosecution for anti-

---

[4] Ibid., p.5.

apartheid activities in South Africa. In the small village of Golema Mmidi he
finds a group of refugees who, like himself, have suffered, endured great griefs
and bitterness, and are trying to make new ordered lives for themselves through
cooperative effort in an agricultural project led by Gilbert Balfour, a young
British agronomist, who likewise dreads the comfort of his emotionally arid
middle-class background. Even old Dinorego and Mma Millipede have earlier in
life suffered as victims of power abuse. Makhaya finally grows out of the hate
which was gradually consuming his being. In Ravenscroft's words:

> Against a political background of self-indulgent, self-owning
> traditional chiefs and self-seeking, new politicians more
> interested in power than people, the village of Golema Mmidi is
> offered as a difficult alternative: not so much a rural utopia for
> the Africa of the future to aim at, as a means of personal and
> economic independence and interdependence, where the qualities
> that count are benign austerity, reverence for the lives of ordinary
> people (whether university-educated experts or illiterate
> villagers), and, above all, the ability to break out of the prison of
> selfhood without destroying individual privacy and integrity.[5]

Head's idealism therefore takes full cognizance of the brutal realism of
the world in which it is meant to be realized. It is pitted against such obstacles
as the long-standing conservatism of the local people and their suspicion of new
techniques; a reactionary chief who is jealous of the cooperative's encroachment
on his traditional privileges, especially that of cattle speculation. Even in this
environment, the personal fears of the participants, their insecurities and the
natural urge to dominate others also have to be fought, for these factors are the
evil which constantly threatens the success of this creative endeavour. The
issues are those of power and identity, and the energy and commitment with
which Makhaya plunges into the venture soon purge him of the disillusionment
and self-destructive hatred with which he first enters the new community. His
eventual union with Paulina Sobeso, a passionate and lonely woman who is also
fleeing a disastrous marriage in northern Botswana, symbolizes this newly found
harmony. However the venture transcends just personal love and harmony for
it also symbolizes harmony between characters of different races, different sexes

---

5 Ravenscroft. "The Novels of Bessie Head", p. 177.

and different ages, as well as the victory of love over oppressive power. Lloyd Brown describes it as "a healing moral growth, reflecting not only the creative purposefulness of individual members but also an unusual degree of harmony between the races and the sexes."[6] Commenting further on Head's moral vision Brown continues:

> ...her moral idealism remains the most powerfully effective and most distinguishing feature of her three novels... Her idealism nurtures her strength as a realistic novelist, enabling her to turn uprootedness into a vantage point from which she scrutinizes social institutions as they usually are--as they distort individual personality through power-oriented definitions of race, sex, religion and individualism.[7]

Head's vision also searches out for complementarity of identities. This complementarity functions either as the necessity for an individual to realize his full potential by recognizing his own in another character who possesses what he himself lacks; or features as two characters functioning as the positive and negative aspects of one person, much in the manner of Dr. Jekyll and Mr. Hyde. Her first novel operates on the first level, while the second type is dramatized in her second and third novels. Makhaya and Gilbert discover this essential unity in their first long conversation; that while Gilbert is running "away" from England, Makhaya is running "into" a settled life with wife and children. "He wanted a few simple answers on how to live well and sanely. He wanted to undo the complexity of hatred and humiliation that had dominated his life for so long." His life had been a battleground for inner conflicts and strifes, and the opportunities at Golema Mmidi gave him the opportunity to put together its fragmented pieces. His sensitivity, trustworthiness, patience and a fascinating ability to make people do his bidding without exerting too much energy are the qualities so clearly lacking in Gilbert, the rational scientist:

> Gilbert was a complete contrast to this wavering, ambiguous world in which Makhaya lived. He was first and foremost a

---

[6] Lloyd Brown, <u>Women Writers in Black Africa</u> West Port: Greenwood Press, 1981, p.164.

[7] Ibid., p. 160.

practical down-to-earth kind of man, intent only on being of useful service to his fellow men. There was nothing fanciful in him, yet the workings of his mind often confused and fascinated Makhaya. It was like one gigantic storage house of facts and figures and plans and intuitive impressions. (WRCG. p.81).

Makhaya appreciates the contrast and decides to adopt an attitude of compromise, considering Gilbert's company and friendship more important than differences in character makeup. From Gilbert, Dinorego, Mma Millipede he imbibes much of human philosophy--the values of generosity, sharing, companionship, forgiveness and positiveness; and finally, "Loving one woman had brought him to this realization: that it was only people who could bring the real rewards of living; that it was only people who give love and happiness" (p. 163). Makhaya's transformation is important to Bessie Head because it once more underscores her belief that the ravages of power can be destroyed if the good in man prevails over the evil in him and if love is posited in place of power. Besides Matenge and other selfish traditional rulers, and such stooges like Joas Tsepe, this destructive element is symbolically represented by the harsh wasteland of Botswana, and by the arresting images of death and decay which Head has given cosmic significance. They all underscore the harsh moral landscape of the novel created by the brutal power of Matenge. The barbed wire-fence which Makhaya successfully crosses over signifies his victory over all the malignant forces ranged against him and all the visionaries in the novel. The combined force of their personal inner powers triumphs over all the obstacles and gives birth to a new social order and new personal values for all the participants. The rebirth is total, and demonstrates the power of creativity over evil; a fact which the beautiful artistic productions of Sobeso's son even while in the grips of drought and consumption amply demonstrate.

Maru, Head's second novel, again integrates the political and the personal in its exploration of the author's vision vis-a-vis power, social and psychological. Maru, the main character, like Makhaya, forsakes the life of fame and importance for love and peace of mind. Head is fascinated by the mystery of human life and the inner strengths buried in the lives of characters like Maru. Brown noticed his fascination when he wrote: "The inner power fascinates Head on another basis. It is intensely individual and private, but at the same time it is the absolute prerequisite in the human form for the achievement of public harmony based on social justice."[8]

Maru is Head's second novel and its complex emotional structure has been commented on in the introductory pages of this essay. In line with the first novel it handles the issues of power and love, now enacted with all the storm and stress that accompany them. It is part of Head's well-known psychological insight that the social and emotional upheaval of this drama are set in motion by Margaret Cadmore, a woman without identity, an outcast in a hostile society whose inner strength, goodness and resilience are pitted against the political power of two totems, born into royalty, feared, respected and pampered.

Both Maru and Moleka not only fall in love with Margaret but undergo drastic character transformation. Maru observed that this powerless woman was the only person in the community who looked him directly in the face. In Moleka's case Maru noticed the "the savage arrogant Moleka was no longer there, but some other person like himself--humbled and defeated before all the beauty of the world" (p.57).

Margaret's internal power derives from her upbringing by her British foster parent from whom she receives a fully strengthened personality which in the great trials and tribulations of her life guarantee the continuance of her inner wholeness and enable her to survive "both heaven and hell." In this situation Margaret feels warmth, love and freedom but with Pete, Seth and Morafi the garish and revolting caricatures and clowns who represent the school at Dilepe to which Margaret was deployed as a teacher, the haunting reality of evil is introduced into the heroine's joy. They constitute the full embodiments of the impersonal and brutal social milieu in which Margaret confronts daily insults from the young and the old; by looks, words and actions. Hers is a life lived between the contest of good and evil, each working by its own form of power.

But the play of power in the context of good and evil is even more subtly explored in the deadly struggle between Maru and Moleka for the love of Margaret. Here lies the central drama of the book whose paradox lies in the fact that the passive heroine indirectly engineers this conflict between two powerful totems just by being herself. Significantly Seth is not offered a choice and never

---

[8] Bessie Head, When Rain Clouds Gather, London: Heinemann Educational Books, 1972), p. 11: Further references to this text will be inserted within the essay.

fully realises the depth of the revenge which she awoke in Maru. As always she takes recourse in her stoicism which had helped her to endure the barbarism and sadism of the society she lives in. It was a feeling of being "permanently unwanted by society." In Maru's hands however she finds herself in company of a visionary and a demon, a lover and a tyrant.

Maru can be seen as the representative individual experimenting on the possibilities of the limitless power which he possesses by virtue of being the hereditary paramount chief-elect of the Botswana, waiting to be installed after his predecessor's death; but rather than exploit the political and social privileges of that position he surprises and shocks the community of Dilepe by giving up these gains in favour of an amorous relationship with an outcast. This choice brings him into collision with Moleka who was Margaret's first love. But Moleka has been his best friend till now, and Head plays their essential oneness throughout the book. In character they possess contradictory traits, positive and negative; each crystallizing in description and action the totality of the personality of the other friend. In fact Ravenscroft goes as far as to ask: "And, are we sure, at the end, that the two chief male characters, Maru and Moleka, who are close intimate friends until they become bitter antagonists, are indeed two separate fictional characters, or that they are symbolic extensions of contending character-traits within the same man?"[9] The new Moleka, who falls in love with Margaret, has more of Maru than of the old Moleka who is arrogant and brutal, but the scheming insensitive Maru is more like the brazen Moleka than the old sensitive Maru, "who had all the stuff that ancient kings and chiefs were made of," the Maru who carries his gods within him (p. 36). He is as unfathomable as Moleka is predictable, yet remains the only one who realizes that it is Moleka's kingdom that was unfathomable:

> It was only Maru who saw their relationship in its true light. They were kings of opposing kingdoms. It was Moleka's kingdom which was unfathomable, as though shut behind a heavy iron door. There had been no such door for Maru. He dwelt everywhere. He'd mix the prosaic of everyday life with the sudden beauty of a shooting star...Moleka was the only person who was his equal. They alone loved each other, but they were

---

[9] Brown, op. cit. p. 168.

opposed because they were kings (Maru, p. 34).

In nothing were their differences of character highlighted as in their attitude to women. Moleka has built himself a most unenviable reputation as an insensitive and sexually exploitative young man. As a result his mother is condemned to spend her life caring for his host of girlfriends and their illegitimate children. In Head's words "Moleka and women were like a volcanic explosion in a dark tunnel. Moleka was the only one to emerge, on each occasion, unhurt, smiling" (p. 35) With Maru it was totally different:

> Maru fell in love with his women. He'd choose them with great care and patience. There was always some outstanding quality; a special tenderness in the smile, a beautiful voice or something in the eyes which suggested mystery and hidden dreams. He associated these with the beauty in his own heart, only to find that a tender smile and a scheming mind went hand in hand, a beautiful voice turned into a dominating viper who confused the inner Maru, who was king of heaven, with the outer Maru and his earthly position of future paramount chief of a tribe. (Maru, p. 35)

It is therefore not surprising that with such heightened sensitivity Maru often took ill after the failure of his love affairs. But Head treats this dichotomy with her usual irony; Maru's methods are cold, calculating and ruthless, the normal methods of those who wield destructive power, the same type he has dissociated himself from by renouncing his chieftaincy and all its political implications. Such an act is in direct opposition to his use of his three spies who sniff, inform and "fix" Maru's plans to tear away Moleka from Margaret. Despite such unorthodox methods of dealing with his rival Head insists that Maru acts according to the directions of the gods he carries within him. It is, after all, another way of exercising power. There is perhaps some logic to Maru's winning of Margaret. The latter possesses that quality of mystery which is part of Maru's make-up, as well as that mine of inner strength and individuality which is her legacy from her British foster-mother, Margaret Cadmore. Bessie Head is exploring a state of moral ambiguity in which most human beings have a bit of the visionary and the demon in them, a balance of good and evil. Maru the schemer is not very different from Moleka, the arch manipulator; and Moleka who loves is not very different from the Maru who walks with gods and goddesses. Margaret symbolizes, in her retention of her love of Moleka, even after her marriage to Maru, Head's ideal woman confronting the issue of male protectiveness, possession on one hand, and male crude power on the other, by a firm sense of choices, which amounts to a demonstration of her own inner power. In other words she is Maru's equal, and as an artist has dreamt Maru's dreams as Maru discovers later to his dismay and joy. Head does not resolve this delicate issue in the course of the story, for despite Maru's overt victory over Moleka his new, almost idyllic life with Margaret has permanently been tainted by a black, boiling cloud, typified by moments of brooding, jealousy and malicious meditation when he wonders whether it was a superior kind of love or a superior kind of power that Moleka had. Whichever one it was he remains lord over the other room in his wife's heart. This presence undermines the degree of his victory, and serves as a constant reminder to him of that dangerous aspect of his personality, the use of ruthless power for selfish reasons which is the true demon that thwarts the effort of visionaries like himself to build a more humane society.

In A Question of Power, Head's power-hungry demon is recreated in the character of Dan. This novel is also her most complex, most ambitious and most profoundly frightening in what it says about the reality of power, loneliness, exile and ultimately insanity. In Ravenscroft's words:

> One wonders again and again whether the phantom world that comes to life whenever Elizabeth is alone in her hut could have been invented by a novelist who had not herself gone through similar experiences, so frighteningly and authentically does it all pass before one's eyes. But there is not confusion of identity between the novelist and the character, and Bessie Head makes one realize often how close is the similarity between the fevered creations of a deranged mind and the insanities of deranged societies.[10]

The novel is set in Motabeng and the events are filtered through the disturbed consciousness of Elizabeth, the central character, who in the process

---

[10] Brown, op. cit. p. 168

of the story undergoes a period of acute inner distress with repetitive cycles of nervous breakdown from which she recovers weaker and more frightened about the world around her. Her hallucinations, fear and obsessive self-doubts are symptoms of her insecurities as a woman and as an outsider in the society. The social discrimination which Margaret suffered among the Botswana in Maru reaches harrowing proportions in Elizabeth's nightmares in A Question of Power, where one of her tormentors never ceases to remind her that she is "a coloured woman." In addition she is frightened of the possibility of running mad like her mother who died in a mental institution where she was locked up for her indiscretion in having a baby for a black stable boy. The principal of her mission school revealed the secret to her when she was thirteen and his prophecy almost came true.

In the unfolding of her solitary mental drama Elizabeth's nightmares are dominated by two characters, Sello and Dan, of whom the former lives in the village of Motabeng, though she does not know him personally. Sello was a crop farmer and cattle breeder. These two characters turn the protagonist's mind into a battleground as they compete for the domination and possession of her personality. Sello is the symbol of love and compassion, elevated to the role of a god or goddess, and who for four years has been "a ghostly, persistent commentator on all her thoughts, perceptions and experiences...First, he had introduced his own soul, so softly like a heaven of completeness and perfection: (p. 14). Sello symbolically appears as a man-like apparition or hallucination sitting in Elizabeth's room at night, constantly revealing to her spiritual truths; "love isn't like that. Love is two people mutually feeding each other" (p. 14). Commenting on Sello's personality the author writes:

> It seemed almost incidental that he was African. So vast had his inner perceptions grown over the years that he preferred an identification with mankind to an identification with a particular environment. And yet as an African, he seemed to have made one of the most perfect statements: "I am just anyone..." It wasn't as though his society were not evil too, but nowhere else could he have acquired the kind of humility which made him free, within, totally unimportant, totally free from his own personal poisons--pride and arrogance and egoism of the soul. It had always been like this, for him--a hunger after the things of

the soul in which other preoccupations were submerged; they
were intuitions mostly of what is right...[11]

In his God-like humility Sello has also transcended the bleak arid
barrenness of the soul which Elizabeth knew so well. He loved not only each
particle of earth around him, but also the natural events of sunrise, including the
people and animals of Motabeng. It was a love which included the whole
universe. Sello had said to himself one evening, "I might have died before I
found this freedom of heart." To Head, "That was another perfect statement, to
him--love was freedom of heart" (p. 11). Sello therefore stands for perfection,
for the God-like in man. In this he is a later development of Maru, and by
inference one of Head's visionaries and a symbol of the good, but he also stands
for evil in a very subtle way.

Dan on the other hand epitomizes destructive male egoism and all that is
vile, personally debasing and obscene. The resultant wild display of wreckage
and power in the form of unbridled eroticism and sexuality constitutes the
greatest threat to Elizabeth's weakened mental health and demonstrates Head's
apprehension of evil and its organic relationship to power. The heroine's
greatest source of torture arises from Dan's ability to violate her mind with his
practised, depraved obscenities. He flaunts before her what Ravenscroft calls
"his gargantuan sexual exploits with an incredible succession of sexually
insatiable females..."[12] Their names: Madam Loose-Bottom, Body Beautiful,
Squelch Squelch, Sugar Plum, The Womb, Miss Pink Sugar-Icing and Miss
Pelican-Beak, to name a few of the seventy-one, are telling enough. Dan's
beastliness and exploitative sexuality remind the reader of Moleka's sexual
abandon and bigotry, and what Head calls "The African man's loose carefree
sexuality which lacks the stopgaps of love and tenderness and personal romantic
treasuring of women" (p. 137). It is to her a frightening aspect of male
domination and abuse of power which by extension manifest themselves in the
oppression of the weak, the lonely and outcasts in most societies of the world.
Dan is literally a tyrant, and he understood the mechanics of power like Hitler
and Napoleon. In his hands, she lives over and over again the torments of

---

[11] Ibid., p. 184

[12] Ibid., p. 184.

mankind's past and present history. To explore the reality of this power-machine in human history Head takes a comprehensive imaginative sweep through world religions, cultures, and myths from Osiris, Medusa, Buddha and even Christ. Through all these Head explores the operations of evil in human affairs, for the question of good and evil is an over-riding concern in this work.

Elizabeth's torments also provide Head with an opportunity once more explore the warring of good and evil in the same individual. The Sello/Dan polarity is a more frightening development of the Maru/Moleka unit in dichotomy theme, and a negation of the Makhaya/Gilbert compromise. It is a polarity which Head never really resolves but rather awakens her reader's awareness of its existence, and points to ways of confronting it. The fact that the God-like Sello has the vicious and vile Medusa of Greek mythology as his alter ego, and that Dan after all, is just an extension of Medusa, underscores the complexity of this reality of the battle between good and evil in the world, and in us. Ironically too, Sello as God remains ambivalent, passive and sometimes overwhelmed by the evil that is his own creation and a function of himself. Sello had created the Dan image to test Elizabeth, as the former informs her after the defeat of Dan. Elizabeth realizes this, or at least suspects this treachery earlier on:

> She could not sort out Sello, the shuttling movements he made between good and evil, the way he had introduced absolute perfection and flung muck in her face. ... His other voice, so quietly, insistently truthful, barely rose above the high storm of obscenity. The two voices often seemed to merge (p.137).

He had been responsible for creating the demons which peopled her nights and threatened to dominate her days too, turning her whole existence into a howling inferno. Yet she felt some affection for the real man, as well as some hatred. He has seen that evil and good travel side by side in the same personality" (p. 98). Elizabeth eventually sees this too, and this recognition heralds her recovery and self-growth," and from the degradation and destruction of her life had arisen a still, lofty serenity of soul nothing could shake" (p. 202). Amidst all her torments and the cesspit which ravaged her soul the only sane centre of purposeful, expanding and hopeful activity in this desolation was the Motabeng Secondary School where she taught, and the agricultural cooperative effort under Eugene, the shining examples of men who have opposed death, evil and greed, and have surrounded themselves with a "creative ferment." These periods offer periodic breaks in her life, which can be described as that of " a person driven out of her own house while demons rampaged within, turning everything upside down (p. 49). Her recovery is a testament of the ability of the human will be to overcome evil after its soul's journey through hell and purgatory.

Bessie Head's three novels demonstrate the unleashing of a powerful imagination, willing to explore the inner recesses of the human personality to explore the significance of power of all forms in its make-up, and to map out the constant warring of the powerful forces of good and evil in each individual. This ambitious philosophical investigation is finally channelled towards the plight of the alienated and helpless individual in society, particularly his plight as an exile from an oppressive regime like that of South Africa. The hope is for a more humane society which she hopes can be achieved only by each individual confronting the horrors of history, as well as the horrors within himself, so that the demons of brute and naked power, cruelty and oppression may not wreck the work of visionaries engaged in the realization of this humane society.

CHAPTER THREE

WOMEN'S ROLE IN HEAD'S IDEAL WORLD

Bessie Head is a crusader for sexual and social justice for all men and women. Her favourite theme is the drama of interpersonal relationships and their possibility for individual growth and regeneration. She explores not only social harmony but also what is unique in each individual who contributes to it. In the realization of this task she employs an imaginative power and an original grasp of style which match her forceful moral vision. In all this, the woman's identity is fundamental; for it is still easy to encapsulate the central issues of all Head's novels into the vital issues of power and identity. In her own words:

> All my work is scaled down to this personality need, with the universe itself seen through the eyes of small, individual life dramas. ("Biographical Notes" A)[1]

She truly approaches her characters as individuals and, with her usual sensitivity and thoroughness, journeys through the inner-most recesses of their lives. The product of this exploration is the emergence of that uniqueness which makes each of them special. To Bessie Head, South Africa typifies power in its ugliest form, and the revulsion with which she views such a moral wasteland has aroused in her a special reverence for human life and dignity.

Head's characters are refugees, exiles, victims, all of whom are involved

---

[1] Bessie Head, "Biographical Notes: A Search for Historical Continuity and Roots: Short paper presented at the Annual International Conference of African Literature, Nigeria, University of Calaber, February 1982.

in a personal and very private odyssey of the soul from which they finally emerge regenerated, as well as spiritually and psychologically enriched. These characters inhabit the harmonious new worlds which operate in her novels; but like Ngugi, she seems to imply that it is only from the interaction of both men and women in relationships of mutual love and respect that such a society can be created. Like Ngugi also she has a number of solid, resilient, and resourceful women in her novels. Through them she explores the limitations of women's roles, their disadvantages and their bruised self-image, and celebrates their occasional successes.

Head saw herself as the paradigm of the African woman struggling against entrenched social and sexual prejudices. As an exile in Botswana, she came to know the realities of alienation, racial prejudice, rejection, and victimization. Although she admitted that her earlier works, When Rain Clouds Gather and Maru, were filled with personal data and responses to challenges that were on the whole internal and private, yet she attained a degree of objectivity which allows her to expose and analyze the problems of the African woman both in the narrow village circle, where she is handicapped by age-old traditional mores and taboos, and in the slightly wider world of the town and the co-operative, where the challenges of a new phenomenon often expose the particular qualities, strengths, and weaknesses of the individual. In most cases these women help to build rather than destroy the harmony which Head is searching for.

Her first novel, When Rain Clouds Gather, deals with the search for roots from different perspectives and as it affects characters of different social backgrounds, with different personal problems. In this first novel three women emerge. They trail the usual characteristics of Bessie Head's women, which normally fall into a pattern of social abuse, emotional trauma, suffering, and finally growth in wisdom, peace, and partial happiness. Although a very important theme in this novel is Makhaya's search for peace and stability within a harmonious social order, his destiny is tightly controlled and eventually resolved by his association with the old woman, Mma-Millipede, and his future wife, Paulina Sebeso. Mma-Millipede has been a victim of the crude and brutal power that Head criticizes in all her novels. She was initially forced into an unwanted marriage with a chief's son, Ramogodi, whom the author describes as "a drunkard and dissipated boaster". Eventually she is divorced by the same Ramogodi, who soon falls in love with his younger brother's new wife and marries her after the offended brother hangs himself. It is part of Head's moral idealism that Mma-Millipede and old Dinorego, whom she was initially prevented from marrying, should finally come together as friendly neighbours. Through her own resourcefulness she soon settles down to a new life in Golema Mmidi. Her early exposure to some amount of missionary education has also impacted on her personality:

> Perhaps Mma-Millipede was one of those rare individuals with a distinct personality at birth. In any event, she was able to grasp the religion of the missionaries and use its message to adorn and enrich her own originality of thought and expand the natural kindness of her heart.[2]

Mma-Millipede emerges from her harrowing experience wiser and more generous. Her kindness and concern for everybody soon make her the mother of all. She watches, counsels the young, and participates in their problems. The young man, Makhaya, is the greatest beneficiary of the old woman's wisdom and love. He has come as a drowning man to a strange community searching for a few simple answers on how to live well and sanely:

> It was to amaze Makhaya after all this that an old woman in the village of Golema Mmidi, named Mma-Millipede, was to relieve his heart of much of its ashes, frustration, and grief. (p.126)

This statement comes after a period of friendship and trust, deliberately engineered and initiated by the old woman, who is partly motivated by her liking for the young man, and partly for the sake of her friend, Paulina Sebeso, who had shown some interest in the refugee. From the old woman Makhaya also learns that generosity of mind and soul is real because the old woman sustains that precious quality at a pitch too intense for him to endure. "He was never to know how to thank her for confirming his view that everything in life depended on generosity" (p.132). Their long conversations yield more fruit than

---

[2] Bessie Head, <u>When Rain Clouds Gather</u> London: Heinemann, 1972, p. 68. Further references to this text can be found within the essay.

the old woman herself ever expected. Mma-Millipede therefore broods over the world of this novel like a guardian spirit, yet operates with the familiar human tools of observation, understanding, kindness, and generosity.

Paulina Sebeso is the other woman who stands out in Golema Mmidi, first on her own merit and personality, and ultimately as the wife of Makhaya. Sebeso, like Mma-Millipede, had an unsuccessful marriage with a Rhodesian man who also killed himself to prove his innocence in a story of official scandal and embezzlement. In the process, she lost a home and all her property, and came to Golema Mmidi with her two children. The motifs of victimization, injustice, and suffering are present in the life of this impetuous and passionate young woman, who is also steadied in her emotional life by Mma-Millipede. Sebeso too learns from her fate, and comes to Golema Mmidi toughened and determined to start a new life. From the start the author sets her apart from the other women around her, for although, according to Head, "she was born into their kind of world and fed on the same diet of thin maize porridge by a meek, repressed, dull-eyed mother" (p.94), even as a child she was very inquisitive and meddlesome. Her athletic ability assured her more education than other women. Even her gait was decisive, and betrayed a sense of direction:

> But through her life she had retained her fresh, lively curiosity and ability to enter an adventure, head first. It was all this that really distinguished her from the rest of the women, even though her circumstances and upbringing were no different from theirs.

> She had travelled a longer way, too, on the road of life, as unexpected suffering makes a human being do.... (p. 94)

Her gift in organization is amply demonstrated in her role at the co-operative. Even the old woman, Mma-Millipede, admits that Paulina is the only woman who can persuade the other women to attend lessons at the farm. Naturally, most of the men find her too bossy. Her courage and strength of character also stand out in her quiet acceptance of the death by tuberculosis of her son, Isaac. The final union of this impetuous woman with the reserved Makhaya marks the end of the refugee's morbid speculations on the oppressors and the oppressed, and his journey towards self-discovery, peace, and happiness.

Dinorego's daughter, Maria, is the third significant female character in this novel. Reserved, clever, and unpredictable, she forms a perfect match to the simple and uncomplicated Gilbert, the practical man and the originator of the little agricultural miracle which is one of the interesting phenomena of this novel. She is soft-spoken and meditative but at the same time full of ruthless common sense. For a long time she has quietly served her father, and after three years she agrees to marry Gilbert whose "strange" ways she reveals to Mma-Millipede when she goes to seek her advice. In her relationship with her husband she remains the dominant personality, quiet but retaining a mind of her own.

Through these women Bessie Head presents us with her ideal; they are all tough, resolute, schooled in suffering, and endowed with shrewd common sense. Their relationship with men is an equal one. They stand out from the generality of Botswana women, whom Head criticizes for acquiescing in their oppression, for remaining their same old "tribal selves, docile and inferior" (p.68) despite their exposure to the opportunity of missionary education. Head laments such a wasted opportunity by women who are naturally disposed to hard work. Nevertheless, her final picture of them remains one of admiration:

> It was always like this. Any little thing was an adventure. They were capable of pitching themselves into the hardest, most sustained labour with perhaps the same joy that society women in other parts of the world experience when they organise fêtes or tea parties. No men ever worked harder than Botswana women, for the whole burden of providing food for big families rested with them. It was their sticks that thrashed the corn at harvesting time and their winnowing baskets that filled the air for miles and miles around with the dust of husks, and they often, in addition to broadcasting the seed when the early rains fell, took over the tasks of the men and also ploughed the land with oxen. (pp.104-5)

In Maru, Head becomes more autobiographical but manages with enough artistic distance to make the history of Margaret Cadmore, named after her British foster mother, a representative one. It portrays the intense racial prejudice and tribal politics which inform life in a Botswana village, and under which women too often become victims. The background story is that of Margaret Cadmore, a Masarwa--the Masarwa are a despised group among the Botswana people--who arrives in the village of Dilepe and becomes the centre of a controversy, not just in the school, but between two friends, both members of the royalty and both in love with her. Insults from children and adults alike fail to discomfit the heroine, since from childhood she has come to live with a feeling of being "permanently unwanted by society." Eventually, the situation is resolved into her marriage to Maru rather than Moleka, whom she loves. She apparently a passive agent in this drama of power. However, she never stops loving Moleka, to the eternal chagrin of her husband, Maru.

Head invests Margaret with an air of mystery which complements Maru's mysterious personality. In addition, Margaret possesses a mine of inner strength and individuality which is her legacy from her British foster-mother. She represents Head's ideal woman, and in her retention of her love for Moleka even after her marriage to Maru, she symbolizes Head's ideal woman confronting the issue of male protectiveness and possession on one hand, and crude male power on the other. In other words, she is Maru's equal and, as an artist, dreams Maru's dreams, as Maru discovers later to both his dismay and joy. This issue is not resolved in the novel. Suffice it that Maru's idyllic married life with Margaret is permanently tainted by a dark boiling cloud, typified by moments of brooding jealousy and malicious meditation.

The victimization of women is further demonstrated in the haste and ruthlessness with which Maru arranges the marriage of Moleka and Dikeledi. Although Dikeledi is born into royalty and has a profession as a teacher in the school at Dilepe she proves incapable of fighting the sexual abuse and arrogance of Moleka, who is notorious for his sexual irresponsibility. Between Prince Ramagodi and Chief Matenge of When Rain Clouds Gather and Moleka of Maru, the image of woman is that of a sexual object to be used and abused at will. Makhaya and Maru, however, stand for the new male humaneness which insists on seeing women as equal partners.

A Question of Power is Head's most complex novel, and her most ambitious. The nature of the emotional and psychological problems of Elizabeth, the main character, is the most obvious aspect of that complexity. It recounts a harrowing experience based on the reality of power, loneliness, exile, and ultimately insanity. In Arthur Ravenscroft's word:

> One wonders again and again whether the phantom world that comes to life whenever Elizabeth is alone in her hut could have been invented by a novelist who had not herself gone through similar experiences, so frighteningly and authentically does it all pass before one's eyes. But there is no confusion of identity between the novelist and the character, and Bessie Head makes one realise often how close is the similarity between the most fevered creations of a deranged mind and the insanities of deranged societies.[3]

The novel is set in Motabeng and the events are filtered through the disturbed consciousness of Elizabeth who, in the process of the story, undergoes severe mental torture, loneliness, fear, and repetitive cycles of nervous breakdown. After each experience she becomes more frightened about the world around her. From her responses and conversations with her tormentors it is easy to identify her hallucinations and fear as the result of her insecurities as a woman and as an outsider in society. Just as in <u>Maru,</u> she is discriminated against and reminded that she is a "coloured woman." All these fears are aggravated by her own personal fear of going mad like her own mother.

In her struggle therefore, the issue of her own identity is primary, because her tormentors have come to regard her mind as a battleground on which each is fighting for the domination of her personality. The obscenities with which Dan violates her mind are to him the surest way of demonstrating his prowess as a man. The catalogue of grotesque women, each identified by a name equally grotesque, is Dan's exhibit of his power. Dan abuses his victim in the manner of all tyrants. Head speaks of Dan's "display of wreckage and destruction." This harassment is a most painful problem for Elizabeth. As she says to Birgitte in confidence and with admiration for Birgitte's nobility of mind:

But mine, my destiny is full of doubt, full of doom. I am being

---

[3] Arthur Ravenscroft: "The Novels of Bessie Head" in <u>Aspects of South African Literature</u> (ed.) Christopher Heywood. London: Heinemann, 1976 p. 184

dragged down, without my willing, into a whirlpool of horrors. I
prefer nobility and goodness but a preference isn't enough; there
are forces who make a mockery of my preferences.[4]

The Motabeng Secondary School where Elizabeth works is the only sane
centre of hopeful activity in the heroine's environment. Birgitte, in her strength
of character and the "stripped-down" simplicity of her goodness," represents
honest human relationships devoid of racial hatred or prejudice. Birgitte, with
her dark unfathomable eyes and her unobtrusive, hidden, and silent manner, is a
direct contrast to the blustering, loud Camilla, who greedily and hungrily draws
all attention to herself and who sees everything in stark black and white; nor
does she, in Elizabeth's words, "see the shades and shadows of life on black
people's faces" (p.82). Such is the variety of women characters in this novel,
but the reader's interest centres on Elizabeth, with all her sorrows, and the
unfolding drama of mental torture in Motabeng village. Like Head's other
women, however, Elizabeth finally prevails; she has come to her journey's end
and attained true self-discovery in her affirmation that "There is only one God
and his name is Man. And Elizabeth is his prophet" (p. 206). In Head's words:

And from the degradation and destruction of her life had arisen a
still, lofty serenity of soul nothing could shake. (p.202)

Head's three novels can be seen as a systematic study of women's roles
and handicaps in society, especially an unjust one like South Africa. She has
also x-rayed their emotional, psychological, and spiritual endowments in the
context of a human society, sane, accommodating. Her women are invariably
thrust into a hostile landscape from which they must grow and realize their
identity. There are passionate women like Dikeledi and Paulina; reserved
women like Maria and Margaret; wise old women like Mma-Millipede; silent
but self-confident women like Birgitte; loud and pushy women like Camilla; and
frightened and mentally tormented women like Elizabeth. Even weird Thoko
has a special value in this landscape. Head assesses the Botswana woman's
worth by the degree of inner strength, individuality, and drive with which she is

---

[4] Bessie Head: A Question of Power. London: Heinmann, 1972, p. 85. Further references to
this text can be found within the essay.

able to rise above the brutalizing and restrictive roles assigned her by an unimaginative society. The degree of humility and sincerity with which she adapts herself to a strange people and society contributes to the harmonious co-existence of all in her environment. In exploring their day-to-day activities Head does not fail to point out that quite often these women perpetuate their own problems through mental conditioning and their acceptance of social norms and taboos and also because of unfounded inter-personal jealousies. For all, their lives are a constant struggle and movement towards self-discovery. The case of Elizabeth in <u>A Questions of Power</u> is the climax of this struggle. That she finally triumphs is a measure of Head's optimism. Elizabeth's victory is marked by her symbolic act of falling asleep and placing her hands peacefully over her land in a gesture of belonging. If there is one fact about Bessie Head that stands out in all her novels, it is her love for the Botswana people, the land of Botswana, and humanity in general.

CHAPTER FOUR

More Than a Metaphor: Nature in Bessie Head's Novels.

Bessie Head's novels are peopled by two groups of living things, man and Nature, one relying so completely on the other that each would remain essentially half-alive without the other. Perhaps because African Literature, especially fiction started with, and explored village life before moving to the town and city novel, it took external Nature as the appropriate environment for its characters and therefore wasted little or no effort in tapping its powerful impact on man, or as a literary tool. In Chinua Achebe's first and third novels with their powerful tragic heroes, reality operates on the levels of man and the supernatural. The thick forests of Umuofia and Umuaro receive no special attention except in so far as they serve as the Evil forest for abandoning twins, people who die of the swelling disease or other serious ailments which the society did not understand; or as the seat of the powerful masquerades respectively.[1] Ezeulu's favourite son, Obika, died in the process of running through the forest as the best way to restore his father's badly--dented reputation! Achebe's works occasionally demonstrate very strongly the working out in human affairs of such fatal irony. But while this irony works itself out external Nature moves along in its own indifferent way. If it occasionally assumes any ominous role in Achebe's work it is only because of the existence of some powerful force within it; the case of Chielo, the priestess of Ani is such

---

[1] Chinua Achebe. Arrow of God. London, Ibadan, Nairobi, Heinemann, 1962.

an abode, meaningful only because it is informed by the numinous presence of the Earth goddess, Ani.

The dark jungles of Amos Tutuola's works are in the same position; lifeless, their beauty and magic uncelebrated; but the satyrs of the jungle dwell in them and give them life. Invariably the impact is a negative one, contributing more to man's woes than to his joys. The forces that stir in the jungle are usually sinister ones. As his heroes journey through them they are subjected to untold hardship and trials; they confront human beings, or animals that behave like human beings; ghosts, in different sexes, sizes and shapes, performing different roles. There are strange gods, demons, ogres and other unimaginable creatures working through spells and magic; for good, but mostly for bad. Eventually the hero or heroine does learn some lesson and does grow in a rigorous bildungsroman fashion. But a brighter sun never joins in celebrating his victory; a heavier and thicker cloud never mourns his loss or joins in his pain. Not even the ever-imminent tropical rain in the forest dares participate in his rite of passage; a ritual of regeneration and the end of a journey typified by a series of nightmarish tests which the hero has undergone to prove himself a better and wiser man, now capable of withstanding all forms of terror, and better equipped to contribute to society in a more positive way. It is a classic theme and the hero is the Yoruba version of Odysseus, Orpheus and Christian. But he operates in a lonely alienated landscape that has no interest in his exploits.[2]

African writers did move slightly towards a semi recognition of Nature at a later date. The novels of Ngugi wa Thiong'o, especially The River Between (1965) furnish some of the earliest examples of this practice, yet the practice remains more of a large symbolic gesture than a Romantic immersion into the wonders and beauty of the bond between man and external Nature. The ridges of Kameno and Makuyu divided by the ever flowing river of Honia are depicted as the symbols of a unity--in division situation where two major groups within a society have existed for years in harmony, until that harmony was shattered by the incursion of a new religion and a new culture--Christianity, which

---

[2] See Amos Tutuola, The Palmwine Drinkard and My Life in the Bush of Ghosts, both published by Faber, in 1952 and 1954 respectively.

condemned basic traditional practices without taking into consideration their significance in the lives of the people.[3] In the wake of the fanaticism, betrayal and violence which grew from this mistake river Honia continues to flow undisturbed in its harmonious way.

In Petals of Blood (1977) which derives its title from a red flower with a visible blemish, Ngugi concentrates on the symbolic significance of that flower as the image of a weaker object attacked and destroyed by a stronger force, in much the same way as the poor workers of Kenya are exploited and abused by their stronger leaders. The famine in the village of Ilmorog which brought untold hardship on the citizens, and the rain which finally marked its end are all symbolic tools in the novel. The rain has also been used as a symbolic tool in Ngugi's A Grain of Wheat (1967) where it assumes the classic cleansing and regeneration roles. One can also find such symbolic application of natural objects like rivers and trees in Ayi Kwei Armah's The Healers (1979), where once more they stand for love, life, regeneration, and oppose the forces of greed, corruption and power.[4] These are the general sweeping trends which have characterised African fiction even as it moves from the expository, demonstrative and sometimes declamatory, to the symbolic.

Bessie Head's attitude to natural objects varies significantly from the above-mentioned ones. She has an eye which searches for some mystery and magic in the tiniest natural objects around her and invests them with some individual worth. They assume life and play roles which ultimately define more meaningfully the activities, motivations and relationships of human beings in her universe which is always a landscape of rich creative ferment dominated by growing individuals.

Bessie Head's three novels are quest novels. They end in self discovery, peace and harmony. In each case a confused or buffeted individual finds love or peace after a gruelling encounter with the forces of societal oppression or the powerful forces within his or her own psyche; what Head calls "personal poisons--pride, and arrogance and egoism of the soul". They all herald the end

---

[3] Ngugi's novel are often organised round a series of symbolic patterns. See especially A Grain of Wheat and Petals of Blood both published by Heinemann.

[4] Ayi Kwei Armah, The Healers is published by Heinemann.

of a journey into the self and a new beginning and blossoming into an enlarged humanity. At the end of <u>Maru</u>, the hero, Maru and his wife Margaret"...were heading straight for a home, a thousand miles away where the sun rose, new and, new each day."[5]   In this context the sun contains within itself the possibility and seeds of its own constant renewal; a renewal which mysteriously permeates the broken lives of individuals in this landscape.

Likewise at the end of <u>When Rain Clouds Gather</u> Makhaya burdened by his dismal train of thought which pays no heed to the "still, glorious ball of hot, red light which hung in the sky:" walks into the warm embrace of his new wife, Paulina.   For them it was a new beginning.   Significantly Makhaya had previously wandered "along the footpath, in the direction of the sunset".[6] The climax of this motif is attained in her third novel, the most ambitious and most personal.   Elizabeth rises from the howling hell of her insanity, from the degradation and near destruction of her life; and towards dawn throws her packet of tablets out of the window as a sign of her new freedom, self-knowledge, and victory over the evil forces that threaten to destroy her:

> She had fallen from the very beginning into the warm embrace of
> the brotherhood of man, because when a people wanted everyone
> to be ordinary it was just another way of saying man loved man.
> As she fell asleep, she placed one soft hand over the land. It was
> a gesture of belonging.[7]

The mending and building up process observed in the lives of Head's characters is one that informs her concept of man and his relationship with the universe he lives in. It cannot but remind the reader of that special bond between external Nature, the spirit of man and the God that dwells in both, which is the hallmark of Wordsworth's poetic theory and practice. In "The

---

[5] Bessie Head. <u>Maru</u>. Nairobi, Ibadan, Heinemann, 1971, p. 125. Further references to this text will be inserted in the essay.

[6] Bessie Head. <u>When Rain Clouds Gather</u>. London: Heinemann, Ed. Victor Gollanez Ltd., 1969. Further references to this text will be inserted within the essay.

[7] Jack Stillinger (ed). <u>Selected Poems and Prefaces</u> - William Wordsworth. Boston: Houghton Mifflin Company, p. 193.

Prelude" Wordsworth writes:

> The earth is all before me. With a heart joyous, not scared at its own liberty, I look about; and should the chosen guide be nothing better than a wandering cloud   I cannot miss my way.

Wordsworth and Head were thankful for the means which "Nature deigned to employ". The seasons, the sun, the moon, a wandering cloud, the craggy ridge, the steams, the birds of the air, the mountain and its echoes, the wind and the rain, darkness and light all were tools of their comprehensive vision of man and the universe.

Bessie Head knew one land, one earth; that of Botswana, her adopted home. She knew her people and their customs, the land and its animals and vegetation, its sights and sounds; and identified with them without reservation. Her works are about ordinary people or important people seeking to be ordinary in an environment where Nature plays a predominant role in the serenity and spiritual fulfilment of such individuals. Such a thorough and sustained exploitation of the ennobling qualities of Nature is noticeable in her three novels. Nature dominates the setting, plots and language especially her imagery; but her attitude is also buttressed by a very practical attitude towards the land, the soil; "a great wonder about the soil and the food it produced", (p.60) she confesses.

Such an attitude to the land has its nearest equivalent in African Literature in East Africa. When Lawino sets off her urgent cry to her husband Ocol:

> Son of the Bull, let no one
> uproot the pumpkin.[8]

it was a cry against the violation of the sanctity of the land. Ngotho and Howland's clash over their individual allegiance and attachment to the land becomes better appreciated within such a context. Head's life-long search for

---

[8] Elaine Campbell. "Bessie Head's Model for Agricultural Reform" <u>Journal of African Studies</u> Vol. 12, No. 2 Summer 1985, p.83

roots both in its literal and figurative sense makes this posture understandable. But in this search and her exploitation of Nature she recognised its double possibilities as friendly and hostile. The drought-stricken land of Botswana was therefore a harsh environment to be tamed. Nature was not always benevolent, it was often "red in tooth and claw;" but Head saw and participated in that challenge, hence the agricultural co-operative community plays a central role in her second and third novels. Golema Mmidi and Motabeng are such communities and Makhaya, Paulina and Elizabeth are their most important psychological beneficiaries. This is why Elaine Campbell insists that these agricultural matters are not Eliot's objective correlative: external equivalents of inner emotional reality. "Instead", she says, "they are subjective correlatives of the human lives with which they are intertwined."[9]

In When Rain Clouds Gather Makhaya finds himself in Baralong village in the winter month of June with its bitter cold wind. He crouches in an old man's hut at dawn counting on the joint conspiracy of the old man and darkness of the night to sprint across the Botswana fence into freedom. The barking of the dog, the chattering of women's voices, music and singing; the loud cry of a child and the laughter of men oblivious of the wall of sirens are important comments on the new life before him. As relief comes near "he noticed how the dust of the mud-floor rose up and shimmered and danced in the sunlight" (p.8). Head calls it "the interweaving dance pattern of the sunlit dust" (p.8) whose almost breathless rhythm eased away his knots of stomach trouble, and he unconsciously smiled to himself. At two strategic moments he says wistfully, "I might like it here". (pp.16, 27). Like Maru he is searching for peace of mind, for a wife and children rather than fame. Like Maru also he follows a dusty little footpath. On his arrival Gilbert, his complementary quest hero tells him, "I like it here", more categorically. It is Gilbert who soon introduces him to the perennial problems of his seemingly idyllic environment, the major blockages to agricultural progress. He was struggling to bring cattle production and crop production together for more effective utilization of crop residues and grain surpluses which would ultimately raise the grade of beef. The country was also

---

[9] Rukmini Vanamali. "A Question of Violence, Maru - A Question of Power". An unpublished paper. University of Calabar.

in the grip of a severe drought, which had already lasted five years and was becoming worse with each succeeding year. In addition:

> ... it was harsh and terrible country to live in. The great stretches of aridland completely stunned the mind and every little green shoot that you put down into the barren land just stood there, single, frail, shuddering, and not even a knowledge of soils or the germinating ability of seeds or modern machinery could help you to defeat this expansive ocean of desert. (p.115).

But Golema Mmidi, a microcosm of Botswana, is also a unique place. Its inhabitants consist of individuals who have fled there to escape the tragedies of life, personal or political. It is named after crop growing, the occupation of the villages rather than after some important chiefs or important events. It is also one of the few areas in the country where people are permanently settled on the land. To crown it all Dinorego was the only full time male crop producer in the village. All the rest are women. Head describes in detail the many natural marvels of this little strip on the eastern side of Botswana. The most amazing is that of the carrot-seed grass "a tough, quick-growing little annual. Its short impoverished leaves grow close to the ground in a spread-out, star-shaped pattern from the centre of which rose a thin stalk, profusely covered by close-packed little burrs". There are also the long, frail feathery stalks of the wind-blown eragrostis, a lush sweet grass. She writes of "other miracles"; varieties of wild flowers, white stars and purple stars, lacy blends of pale-pink blossoms, jaunty yellow-gold of strange freakish daisies. All this strange new growth fired Gilbert's imagination, enthusiasm and expertise. But this is the year when September came and no rain clouds gathered as has been the practice. It is the year of death of cattle, and of Paulina Sebeso's son in the cattle outpost. Gilbert called the death of the cattle a miracle for it hastened his experiment of turning Golema Mmidi into "a farmer's heaven". It also proved Makhaya "the magician who could make tobacco co-operatives appear overnight". (p.155).

This transformation of the landscape is more than a metaphor for the transformation of the lives of the characters involved in it. It is a reality put into practical application and which Head believes cloaks one of the wonders and mysteries of human life. Her descriptive passages clearly demonstrate this belief. Paulina's thoughts are described "as uncertain and intangible as the blue smoke of the fires which unfurled into the still winter air and disappeared like vapour." (p. 94). Gilbert too is described in similar terms. "... everything the unusual Gilbert did seemed to be harmonious and acceptable like the sunrise and sunsets" (p. 94). His life "... was like all the rivers and sunsets and the fish in the rivers and the trees and pathways and sun and wind". (p.86). Maria summarises this phenomenon at the height of the drought

> "You may see no rivers on the ground but we keep the rivers inside us. That is why all good things and all good people are called rain. Sometimes we see the rain clouds gather even though not a cloud appears in the sky. It is all in our heart." (p.168).

Paulina's love is described as a "warm sun" on all the the shadows of Makhaya's life. Her sunset skirt of bright orange and yellow flowers underscores this sun imagery. Their impending union is encapsulated in the drama of the kidney-bean-shaped seeds, an act loaded with phallic symbolism:

> One evening Makhaya walked into a great thorn drama. The thornbrush was seeding and it did this in a vigorous way. One spray of seed struck him on the cheek, and on a closer inspection, he noticed that all the branches were profusely covered with bean-like pods. These pods twined tightly inward until they were coiled springs. He stretched out his hand, broke off a pod and pressed it open. A few minutes kidney-bean-shaped seeds slithered on to his palm. (p.78).

Paulina significantly watches as Nature celebrates with man the impending primordial act of procreation. This union heralds the total transformation of the wavering ambiguous world of the erstwhile bitter and brooding young man into a future characterised by love, peace, harmony and personal satisfaction. Paulina too is rewarded for years of agony in an unhappy marriage.

Under this revitalising umbrella of Golema Mmidi, Old Dinorego, Mma-Millipede, Gilbert and Maria all find their dreams fulfilled and their lives enriched through love, marriage and communal activities in which all the strange new growth which for years lay dormant in the soil also comes alive.

Maru, the second novel, begins from the end. The hero has come to the end of his search and now suffers from the guilt of his marriage accomplished through cold intrigue, intimidation, ruthless scheming and exercise of brute force.

> Maru had violently broken the unspoken sentiment of love between Margaret and Moleka, and therefore though he is the victor now, the memories of the past cast ominous shadows on his mind and heart and turn him into a tyrant. [10]

In recounting the touching romantic tale of Maru's and Margaret's love the author looks at Nature and sees the hot, dry summer with the black storm clouds that "clung in thick folds of brooding darkness along the low horizon" as an unmistakable sign of the hero's ambiguous victory. In Head's words the clouds " ... were not promising rain. They were prisoners, pushed back, in trapped coils of boiling cloud." (p. 5). Maru is Head's ideal man; " ... one long accustomed to living in harmony with the earth". He has run away from fame; he has rejected the road to power and the unbridled privileges of the Totem. He has shocked Dilepe village by touching an untouchable, and is now occupied preparing his garden of yellow daisies, "because they were the only flowers which resembled the face of his wife and the sun of his love". (p. 1). He is involved in a creative benign action which belies a far-reaching political statement. His choice of a Masarwa wife, an outcast, and his own austere life of isolation and integrity; of willingly wresting a precarious living from the soil of a new locale once more bring us to Head's reverence for the soil. The political significance of this marriage notwithstanding its spiritual and creative possibilities send a thread of meaning started in Head's first novel to be enlarged in the third. Maru's godlike perspicacity is often emphasised, for after all he carries his own gods within himself and those voices had chosen his path for him, we are told. Throughout this romantic cum political story Nature and its effects on man's mind and life predominate. The usual dusty footpath, dancing yellow daisies, the thorn tree and parched white grass of her earlier

---

[10] Elaine Campbell, op. cit. p. 83.

novel are easily recognisable. So close is Maru's bond with Nature that "there had never been a time in his life when he had not thought a thought and felt it immediately bound to the deep centre of the earth, then bound back to his heart again--with a reply." (p. 7). He is therefore the priest elect and the mythical superman. But he believed that there was "a clear blue sky in his mind that calmly awaited the storm in his heart." (p. 8). This phenomenon would wash away all he hated from the face of the earth. But a dark shadow permanently created a balance in their Edenic love affair because the law of Nature has been broken.

The older Margaret Cadmore was responsible for giving Maru this wife whose eyes are "as pretty as stars". "She was a little bit of everything in the whole universe because the woman who had educated her was the universe itself." (p. 20). In Dilepe village another magical act occurs between Moleka and Margaret as "a rainbow of dazzling light" quickly clears the "stormy sky" which the former had been identified with. Her new found love is compared to a "rising sun". In Moleka's new experience:

> Perhaps it was only this - the light in the sky and the quietly glittering beauty of the earth which matched a portion of his body that felt like a living pulsating sun. (p. 31).

The irresponsible and often callous Moleka, the `casanova' of Dilepe finds himself in the power of a reality neither he nor his mother could understand. Elizabeth claims in A Question of Power that "Love is so powerful, it's like unseen flowers under your feet as you walk." (p. 86).

Their love is called a river with a permanent flow and in its grip Dilepe became hallowed ground, and Moleka fell in with the usual sunrise and sunsets of Head's world. Even in Margaret's painting "a half-sun gazed with a glowing eye into her heart", (p. 113) and to herald Margaret's marriage to Maru the constellations shift their positions in the sky. (p. 124). The most profound statements spiritual and political about human relationships and the mysteries of the individual soul are consistently made through the vehicle of natural phenomena. That is why the inscrutable power of Moleka remains frozen behind his "thunder-cloud brow". The strange machinations and gymnastics of the Queen of Sheba and Windscreen-Wiper seal this abiding alliance and harmony among all levels of God's creation. Sheba even dies in order that Margaret may live.

The social and humane revolution at the end of <u>Maru</u> embraces even the despised Masarwa as one of their own marries into royalty:

> ... a door silently opened on the small, dark, airless room in which their souls had been shut for a long time. The wind of freedom, which was blowing throughout the world for all people, turned and flowed into the room. As they breathed in the fresh, clear air their humanity awakened. (p. 126).

Characteristically their freedom is symbolised by the wind, and the sun. "They started to run out into the sunlight", away from their accustomed dark room.

No where in Bessie Head's works is the healing, liberating and regenerative power of Nature on human life better demonstrated than in her third novel, <u>A Question of Power</u>. The book is about growth of food and growth of human life. Says Head:

> It is impossible to become a vegetable gardener without at the same time coming into contact with the wonderful strangeness of human nature. Every man and woman, is in some way, an amateur gardener. (p. 72).

These lines surprisingly issue from a text which is dominated by the story of the heroine's series of mental breakdown, her hallucinations and nightmarish existence between fantasy, insanity and reality. These horror filled experiences are generated by two overpowering masculine figures, Dan and Sello whose schemes can ultimately be reduced into the perennial battle between good and evil in the life of every human being. At the end, the heroine emerges victorious, affirms her own identity as a woman and as a free human being and citizen of the world.

Head's own life in the Botswana agricultural community informs this novel and restores her sanity. As usual the setting is a little village in Botswana populated by a medley of exiles, foreign agricultural helpers and local men and women. This world forms a total contrast to the howling inferno which

Elizabeth lives in most of the time. It is a seat of love, understanding, and sharing. Most of all it is a wonder of Nature. The garden dominates the book in reality and as a motif. It performs a creative function. Unfortunately, "if such a beauty and harmony built up in her outward circumstances it was at total odds with the tormented hell of her inner world." (p.157). The magic of this garden is underscored by the harsh and hostile landscape of Motabeng:

> Motabeng means the place of sand. It was a village remotely inland perched on the edge of the Kalahari Desert. Seemingly the only reason for people's settlement there was a good supply of underground water. It took a stranger some time to fall in love with its harsh outlines and stark black trees. (pp. 19-20).

This deprived landscape becomes the new home of the Cape Gooseberry. The "miracle" first occurs in Elizabeth's yard. But as it spread:

> The work had a melody like that - a complete stranger like the Cape Crooseberry settled down and became a part of the village life of Motabeng. (p. 153).

> So tobacco, tomatoes, broccoli, peanuts all grew happily side by side in her garden. Tobacco was for snuff, peanuts for cooking oil and peanut butter, tomatoes were `specialities' and broccoli might just like to grow in Motabeng. (p. 163).

These "feeling" "thinking" vegetables are just a few in her natural garden world of crisp, juicy leaves of Swiss Chard, Collards from America and perpetual spinach beet", carrots, pumpkin and barley: Together they form a microcosm of what Campbell calls "a possible agricultural reform in Africa, a seed packet for a continent".[4]

A parallel action and similar transformation also occur in the lives of the characters involved in this project: Eugene the man, Kenosi, Kepotho, Small-boy, Tom. Mrs. Jones and "The half-mad Camilla woman", who always exclaimed about nature, but is now subdued, all find fulfilment economically and psychologically. This is why Campbell can confidently assert that

More than an objective correlative, more than an image, a

metaphor, or even a symbol, Elizabeth's vegetable garden is her
link with the community, her therapeutic outlet, her actualization
of a woman's worth, her contribution to the brave new world of
equitable human relationships (p. 83).

The garden in all its ramifications provides the positive forces that
finally triumph over the veiled brutality of Sello and the vicious sexual
obscenities of Dan and Medusa. At the end of Part One Nature affirms its
supremacy:

> The dawn came. The soft shifts and changes of light stirred with
> a slow wonder over the vast expanse of the African sky. A small
> bird in a tree outside awoke and trilled loudly. The soft, cool air,
> so fresh and full of the perfume of the bush, swirled around her
> face and form as she stood watching the sun thrust one powerful,
> majestic, golden arm above the horizon. (p. 100).

More significant is her symbolic act at the end of Part Two:

> As she fell asleep, she placed one soft hand over her land. It was
> a gesture of belonging; (p. 206).

for "from the degradation and destruction of her life had arisen a still, lofty
serenity of soul nothing could shake" (p. 202).

Bessie Head's novels can be regarded as regional novels because they are
all set in a little drought-stricken country she lived and died in. Although she
was South African by birth, Botswana was the only home she called her own.
She also wrote about the persona she knew best, herself; and the people she
knew best, the rural Botswana and the team of foreign friends and exiles who
inhabited that land. In their midst she partially found the roots she searched for
all her life: the soul of Botswana, the rural scenes, its sparsely furnished huts,
its agricultural and pastoral rhythm, its animals, food and birds all gave her a
sense of history, of destiny, of roots. Head once spoke of her "reverence for
human life" but forgot to mention her reverence for external nature, its beauty,
its wonder, its magic which provided `pockets of peace' and growth for the
human psyche.

In anchoring her novels so solidly on the common place, people and

Nature she has broken new grounds in a literary tradition so bent on making political and cultural statements that the abounding possibilities of the natural environment are often totally ignored. Head has given African literature new themes; experimented on a new source of inspiration. Although her works lack any recognisable articulated doctrine on the innumerable benefits of Nature her thematic and moral concerns amply point to her belief in a Nature which is primarily a background of delight, a means of spiritual exaltation, one capable of healing disillusionment and rootlessness, leading back to peace and understanding, spiritual poise and strength. Perhaps no poet has felt the presence of Nature as deeply as Wordsworth who had claimed that it can "breathe/grandeur to the very humblest face/of human life". Although Wordsworth's best poetry, like Bessie Head's, revolves around himself, his deepest personal concerns reach out to the whole body of Nature and to his fellow creatures contained within her embrace. The joint community of man and Nature is the core of Head's new world.

In Golema Mmidi and Motabeng she watched and lived with people who believe in patterns of goodness; in tenderness, especially tender heavens of compassion, as she describes it. She set out to celebrate the intangible, unpraised efforts people of different backgrounds made to establish the brotherhood of man in a landscape suffused with natural and moral beauty. It was not always perfect; just nearly so; but it took in its expansive embrace man and the whole of nature. In celebrating this almost mystical union with exquisite poetry Bessie Head also found her own ultimate freedom, for a poet has described freedom as, to give "one's self, time and knowledge" to the service of one's fellow men.

CHAPTER 5

HEAD AS STORY TELLER AND HISTORIAN

Bessie Head's literary enterprise has a grand design. I call it an enterprise because it was undertaken with the plan and seriousness of a great adventure; as a challenge, and with determination to plunge into an undertaking of permanent ramifications. That grand enterprise was to capture imaginatively the mystery, magic and wonder of life, and the universe in general through a recreation of a small southern African country, Botswana. Bessie Head's love of Botswana and its people is a reality she articulated so often that four years after her death, and with all the critical writings on her life and works, a listing of such comments is no longer a necessity. However one example should suffice.

> In my eyes Botswana is the most unique and distinguished country in the whole of Africa. It has a past history that is unequalled anywhere in Africa. It is a land that was never conquered or dominated by foreign powers and so a bit of ancient Africa, in all its quiet and unassertive grandeur, has remained intact there. It became my home in 1964![1]

But to one with Head's terrifying life history the word "home" means much more than it does to the ordinary person who basically conceives of home as a place of love, warmth, security and understanding. Head was born into a nightmare and Botswana as a home lifted from her that nightmare sense of

---

[1] Bessie Head, "Social and Political Pressures that shape Literature in Southern Africa" Cecil Abrahams (ed.) <u>The Tragic Life</u>. Bessie Head and Literauture in Southern Africa. Trenton N.J. Africa World Press, 1990, p. 12.

despair. (Head, 1990). Bessie Head always lamented the fact that South Africa made its black people just objects of abuse and exploitation, and stripped them of a sense of worth. The destiny was already worked out before the individual was born and became harsher and harsher as time progressed. She was concerned that South Africa as a land offered the world only gold; "no great men were needed to articulate the language of the people" (Head 12). Head considered it a land long lost, a world that never seemed meant for humans in the first place, a world that reflected only misery and hate. In a creative sense she saw it as her duty and that of future generations to answer the questions posed by such an unnatural environment. In her usual sincerity and self-effacement she confessed what obstacles such a situation constituted to her creativity:

> I cannot pretend to be a student of South African Literature. I cannot assess its evolution or lack of evolution. I only feel sure that the main function of a writer is to make life magical and to communicate a sense of wonder. I do admit that I found the South African situations so evil that it was impossible for me to deal with in creative terms (The Tragic Life, p.13).

Botswana provided the answer to her questions and gave birth to a bout of creative activity which produced three accomplished novels, a book of short stories and a quasi historical-mythic account of the same society. Through them she has covered the whole spectrum of Southern African preoccupation--"refugeeism, racialism, patterns of evil and the ancient South African historical dialogue". Although all her works have Botswana settings it is understandable that the range and reach of such preoccupation became very wide. Says Head, "People, black people, white people, loomed large on my horizon. I began to answer some of the questions aroused by my South African experience" (The Tragic Life, p.13). In her grand literary design therefore she covered all aspects of the land and people of the country; but the magic was always foremost in her mind:

> With all my South African experience I longed to write an enduring novel on the hideousness of racial prejudice, but I also wanted the book to be so beautiful and so magical that I as the

writer, would long to read and re-read it. (The Tragic Life, p.14).

Head made the above comments in connection with <u>Maru</u> (1971) but they easily apply to all her works, including the over-powering <u>A Question of Power</u> (1974) in which she undertook, in her own words, "a private philosophical journey to the sources of evil." In unveiling that magic she blended fact with fiction; there is room for history, fantasy, dreams, myth, legend and even witchcraft. This is an attempt to locate the positions and roles of her two works of non-fiction in her creative universe.

<u>The Collector of Treasures</u> (1977) is Head's fourth book, a group of thirteen short stories in which she concentrates on the human treasures of the past, present and future which were ignored or not fully explored in her novels. Nigel Thomas has called Head's stories "an intensification, a distillation, if you will, of Botswana history and actuality in order to suggest its impact on those who live it". (<u>The Tragic Life</u>, p.93) These stories deal with the same themes and reveal the same artistic mastery with which the novels were written, and also betray the same moral concern for a better world, by praising good and condemning all forms of evil and oppression as the novels do. In their ever refreshing and simplified form her stories reflect a deep understanding of human actions and motives. Besides this complementary role to the novels, her short stories contrast with the novels in a subtler way; that of shifting her attention to what Ojo-Ade calls " the common beings of her community". (<u>The Tragic Life</u>, p.80) Her novels cover the lives and concerns of Botswana royalty, chiefs, school teachers, missionaries, enlightened agriculture graduates, political activists and exiles as well as wise and respected elderly Christian leaders in the community. In the stories we come face to face with the mostly illiterate village population. Whereas characters in the novels are fired by a general awareness of their problems and a commitment towards an improved emotional, social and economic state, Head speaks for her characters in the stories in the oral tradition which reflects their particular environment and special problems. In this setting the author goes back into that past whose ancient wisdom and practices now live in the pages of oral poetry and narrative as the present fast erodes their validity. She recreates for us the lives of those whom the "short anonymous-looking"

missionary in the first story considers the silent mass of humble and lonely who had an almost weird capacity to creep quietly through life" (The Collector of Treasures p.10) Notice the quiet strength with which the young couple, Ralokae and Galethebege, under the tutelage of the old man Modise choose a traditional wedding despite the threat of Christian damnation. This is why Ojo-Ade writes:

> The style, simple and down-to-earth finds is characters with ease,
> the down-trodden, the desolate, the defeated, all non-heroic due
> to their estate but heroic as the centre of concern of the writer
> and, in several cases as courageous commoners. (The Tragic
> Life, p.80)

Besides her unveiled criticism of the insensitivity and bigotry of missionaries who have contributed to the destruction of traditional norms of behaviour, Head concentrates on the family as the nucleus of the society. To comment on the quality of family life and the near destruction of that institution she goes back to her favourite "individual life dramas" which dot the world of her novels and non-fiction. The thirteen stories deal with different stages, aspects and problems of family life with a clear concentration on the role of the woman. Head's impatience with the sexual ruthlessness and irresponsibility of Botswana men are amply dramatised in the escapades of Moleka. (Maru, p.19) Side by side with such men are the docile, sometimes foolishly long-suffering women whose lives they destroy. The stories therefore present us with a two-sided world of communal sharing and togetherness in joy and sorrow as well as an exploitative immoral and often violent contrast. The romantic tale of Sebembele and Rankwana is posited as the ideal. Like Maru, the man Sebembele sacrifices inheritance and goes into exile with the woman he loves and their baby.[2] Significantly Rankwana was the youngest wife of his now dead father. The extreme of this type of self-sacrifice can be found in the story of Rose, the beautiful woman who devotes her life nursing her blind and not-so-responsible husband, Gobosamang (Kgotla). This tale however demonstrates the maturity and complexity of Head's vision even in these seemingly simple stories. The issue of one sided devotion is central; that of jealousy is another

---

[2] Bessie Head. The Collector of Treasures. London: Heinemann, 1977, Further references to the text will be inserted in the essay.

and the third is the fact that proximity of background in a marriage does not necessarily ensure a successful marriage. Finally, is Rose too good to be believed? But Head forestalls the reader's scepticism by first letting Kelapibe proclaim Rose a wonder, and secondly by isolating her as a foreigner. Head knew that the perfect character, in life and in literature, is always a bore. Such an attitude makes her characters both types and individuals and lodges her stories within the realistic tradition.

Man and woman in the family form the centre of Head's stories but most of the time man emerges as the inconsiderate destroyer and cause of misery, typified by a form of behaviour which has also turned the women into hard callous partners equally lacking in tenderness. In Mabeboge's words, "I lost...because women are just dogs in this society" (p.81)

Head's harshest words for such men come in the central story "The Collector of Treasures". Sebembele belongs to the little minority:

> The majority created such misery and chaos that he could broadly be damned as evil...That kind of men lived near the animal level and behaved with the same. Like the dogs and bulls and donkeys he also accepted no responsibility for the young he procreated and like the dogs and bulls and donkeys he also made females abort (Collector, p.91)

Head holds them responsible for the complete breakdown of family life. This story ends in an open condemnation of the tribal order which nurtured such practices and such men; and the colonial one which aggravated them by separating working men from their families. The attendant resentment and emptiness were logically turned into mindless destruction and violence on the helpless woman at home. Garesego Mokopi was such a man and Dikeledi was the victim, and Head blames the ancestors for their failure and cruelty:

> The ancestors made so many errors and one of the most bitter-making things was that they relegated to men superior position in the tribe, while women were regarded, in an congenital sense, as being an inferior form of human life. To this day, women still suffered from all the calamities that befall an inferior form of human life. (Collector p.192)

It is an aspect of Head's broad-minded philosophy of life that she also sees Makopi as the victim of the South African social and economic system in which he is nothing but a "boy" and comes back to his family "a broken wreck with no inner resources at all". His cruelty and oppression of his wife are simply his effort to flee his own inner emptiness.

Head's feminist tirade in this story and the tragic consequences of the consistent abuse of women are fully illustrated by the final determination of Dikeledi to punish her sex maniac of a husband. She turns on the irresponsible Mokopi and murders him for four steady years of abuse and degradation. To crown it all, in jail Dikeledi meets three other women serving jail terms for similar offences. These women have literally castrated their husbands for their sexual misdemeanours, and show no remorse for their actions. Head obviously has some admiration for such women who after such a period of unmitigated suffering decide to avenge themselves and assert their humanity even in such extreme form. They form the complete contrast to Rose who sacrifices her whole life to serving her blind but treacherous and irresponsible husband; she forgives his infidelity, pays back his debt and withstands his ceaseless complaints. Nigel Thomas and Ezenwa-Ohaeto have dealt in detail with Head's narrative technique of conflation of different stories, of the use of contrastive characters and events for artistic and didactic purposes. Paul Thebolo falls into this technique. His generosity in adopting Dikeledi's three children and welcoming Dikeledi herself into their family serve as Head's illustration of her paradigm among men. Like Maru, like Sebembele, he is Head's new humane man:

> There was another kind of man in the society with the power to create himself anew. He turned all his resources, both emotional and material, towards his family life and he went on and on with his own quiet rhythm, like a river. He was a poem of tenderness. (p.93)

In Head's typical language he is connected with rivers, sunlight and shadows, symbolic of regeneration, recreation; always self-sustaining. Thebolo stands for peace, love and tenderness. Head has eyes for other types of women as Ma-Mompati who walked about with her bible but domineered over and exploited her husband and son until the latter finally asserted his freedom. She is however not as terrible as the priest, Lebojang who used the word of God to hide his series of ritual murders. There is also Life, another important heroine.

The ironic and symbolic name of this city girl once more brings out Head's consummate artistry in these stories. Life brings back from the city the destructive forces which lead to her own tragic death in the village. In the city she had been a singer, beauty queen, a model and a prostitute. She was a new thing to the villagers. Although the other women mainly, farmers, bar tenders, teachers and nurses slightly envied her for the bits and pieces of foreign culture she brought from the city "what caused a stir of amazement was that Life was the first and only woman in the village to make a business out of selling herself. (p. 39). And so in the almost medieval confrontation of virtue and vice, Lesego, her husband, symbolising death, walks into her bar: He was the nearest thing she had seen for a long time to the Johannesburg gangsters she had associated with--the same small economical gestures, the same power and control". (p.41). The meeting and eventual marriage between Life and the respected cattleman ends in the death of the reckless young woman from the city, recalling Head's original symbolic statement: "Then one evening death walked quietly into the bar. It was Lesogo, the cattle-man" (p. 41) The ultimate irony of the tragic relationship is that Life was the first woman with whom Lesogo, known for his transient encounters with women, was willing to settle down. Ojo-Ade has more to say on this irony:

> As usual in a Bessie Head story, and with an irony made all the more mind-boggling by scientific and sexual coupling, like poles repel. The good woman is forever seeking after the bad man; the good man, always attracted to the bad woman...A further twist in the whole logic of science translated into human irony by Bessie Head is, that both qualities of good and evil are at once present in each of the two protagonists of the tragic drama. (p.86)

Sianana, Lesogo's friend, summarises it in folk wisdom; "There are good women and good men but they seldom join their lives together". (p.46) Head therefore portrays the style brought by Life to the village as truly life-denying and demeaning, and a total contradiction of all that the village holds highly. Yet this is not a denial of the value of change but rather an advocacy of the positive aspects of modernism; to allow the preservation of what is also positive within the indigenous culture; the blending of both makes for Head's morally healthy and humane society which accords dignity to all.

In Head's novels marriages are contracted after painful emotional experiences which prepare the couples for the accompanying joys, trials and tribulations. Paulina Sebeso recovers from the trauma of her first unfortunate marriage and finds love and respect in Makhaya's hands. Dikeledi and Moleka; Maru and Margaret also enter marriage contracts yet to be tested. In the short stories, Head concentrates on established relationships and analyses why most of them have been fraught with pain and disappointments. Within this context of marriage in these stories, individuals are seen battling the conflicts with Christianity and western values that are gradually eroding traditional beliefs and practices. They challenge unjust traditional customs with varying degrees of success. Hypocrisy, greed, exploitation, victimization of the weak by the strong and abuse of any form of power are criticised. The stories therefore make social and political comments for the improvement of society and the fulfilment of individuals that live in it. That is the essence of Head's world, a world of harmony.

Serowe: Village of the Rain Wind was published in 1981. Although written in a non-fictive form it bears in different configurations the usual Bessie Head themes, attitudes and emphasis displayed in her novels and short stories, for neither growing fame not maturing talent ever destroyed the abiding wonder and indescribable appreciation with which she touched, talked and wrote of human life and its sanctity. Man, woman, the young and the old, ruler and ruled are all precious in the special magic which each brought to the rhythm of life, inspite of hardships, injustice, poverty and political oppression. But the ordinary held the greatest fascination for her; ordinary people and their ordinary actions; the ordinary motions of nature which were part of her daily life in Botswana, especially in Serowe which is the capital of Botswana and its microcosm in various ways. With its mixture of indigenes, foreign experts and exiles the human landscape of Botswana presented her with sufficient examples of human histories to dramatise the harmony between people and the environment which she believed in so deeply. They dominate the narrative spaces in her writings where each is treated with her avowed respect for the magic of human life.

In the fictive discourse of her novels she speaks for them, reconstructing and reclaiming for them lost dignity, lost hope and lost pride; transforming their lives of agony and dispossession into songs of personal freedom. She, the supreme exile, fighter and dreamer writes:

> I foresee a day when I will steal the little of God, the unseen Being in the sky and offer it to mankind. From then onwards people as they pass each other in the street each day will turn to each other and say, "Good morning, God." War will end. Human suffering will end.
>
> I am building a stairway to the stars. I have the authority to take the whole of mankind up there with me. That is why I write.[3]

Here, as in many other instances, she demonstrates the selfless ability to transcend her personal experience of alienation and abuse, and embrace a universal redemptive role for humanity in general.

In <u>Serowe</u> she continues to collect these same human treasures, but chooses to relinquish the role of the bard and folk story - teller for a more objective posture. In this work she is historian and ethnographer, a chronicler completing for the world the panoramic history of the small community of Serowe with its "ancient African ways" and other practices, a task which she began in the novels and short - stories. She no longer mediates between character and audience, but rather revitalises her discourse with the injection of over a hundred voices narrating personal life histories and commenting on various aspects of the life of this semi-arid country which fired and mertured Head's creative genuis for many years. Occasionally she mixes historical commentary of her own with the individual statements and accounts from the villagers themselves, thus achieving a feeling of immediacy and verisimilitude. At the end one is left with a landscape full of personal profiles and a sense of the historical movement of their time. While celebrating cultural cohesion there is an acceptance of change and progress and the improvement it has brought to

---

[3] Linda Susan Beard. "Bessie Head's Syneretic Fictions: The reconceptualization of Power and the Recovery of the Ordinary" <u>Modern Fiction Studies</u> Vol. 37, No. 3, 1991, 9.580.

individual lives and the community as a whole. <u>Serowe</u> celebrates social plenitude and interaction between indigenes and foreigners. It is the factual part of her fiction, the conclusion of her story.

<u>Serowe</u> is also the story of a struggle. The voices of the members of the different brigades testify to this fact. Besides demonstrating the achievements in the various creative, educational and technical projects by men an women, this multi-pronged development project often exposes the problems of a small community caught at the crossroads of an ancient culture, and a new one, disruptive as well as beneficial. With reference to the Swaneng Project we read:

> The brigades are possibly the most interesting aspect of all the work done so far on the Swaneng Project. They are small factory units and slowly they build up a labour force, for as yet unrealised industrial development. They are both a delight and a pain. Brigade work is at a present delight, its character is creative, haphazard and as yet unconfined in any formal, technical institution. Brigade work is done anywhere--in rough tin sheds, under trees and in roughly made low-cost buildings. It is an endless delight to eat an egg or a chicken, or purchase a woolen blanket that silently bears the stamp: Made in Serowe. (Serowe, p. 146)

Apart from such generalised attitudes and feelings towards Botswana and its mixed population, Head isolates the history of Serowe as the profile of a typical traditional African village whose destiny is bound up with the lives of three important personalities, Khama the Great, Tshekedi Khama and Patrick van Rensburg. She tells the story through the contribution of these men to the community and the response of the community to their ideas and ideals. Like Head's ideal heroes they are vast and spiritually rich personalities. They believed in education and social reforms. Khama's christianizing mission is a major part of these reforms; its outcome was commitment, service, endurance and sacrifice both from the villagers and from strangers like van Rensburg whose doggedness gave birth to all the schools in Serowe up till that time. Despite occasional traces of nostalgia from the accounts of the elderly, there is a steady transformation into a more progressive, better educated society based on the dreams of three great men:

> The three men are all of the same kind. They wanted to change the world. They had to make great gestures. Great gestures have an organic effect on society--they flood a whole town. (Serowe, XV)

But of Patrick Van Ronsburg she writes:

> He has an air of impersonal abstraction, the legend and the fame. The legend was his diplomatic position in South Africa and his abdication from that position on moral grounds. In later years the fame of his educational theories for developing countries spread far and wide. Part of the legend is almost inaccessible as it is personal; in his writings he seems to lack the gift of self-revelation, or perhaps the personal is relegated to some unimportant backroom of his life. Had he been a Tolstoy we might have had *My Confession* and *What I Believe*, in relation to that tortuous country, South Africa. What we do have is an obscurely written semi-autobiography, *Guilty Land*, which deals with and dismisses his life in South Africa. while his major writing talents (and they are prolific) have been deflected into the production of new educational theories, project work and rural development. (Serowe p.35)

Head's admiration for these men is supported by some of her story tellers. Thato Matome, a school teacher, is so overwhelmed by what she regarded as the God-like dignity of Tshekedi Khama, his quiet, modest, gentle, and at the same time magnetic way that she produces a letter Khama wrote her apologising for failing to reply to all her letters and inviting her to visit his new home. But like most leaders he also had enemies who held him responsible for the breakdown of family life with the attendant problems which followed Khama's imposition of Christianity on a people who had for long relied on the securities offered by customs. Head's admiration for its leaders is a small part of her love for Serowe as a place with a character, which time and time again is referred to. She describes her women as "serious, intent, kind, genial,

accommodating, reserved with now and then a flicker of humour" (p.83). In
another place she writes:

> Serowe is a traditional African village with its times and seasons
> for everything; the season of plouging, the season for weddings,
> the season for repairing huts and courtyards and for observing the
> old moral taboos (p.XI)

That Head fell perfectly into this pattern is evident in the manner in
which she isolates its togetherness as its most endearing quality. It was there she
finally settled down, found the ultimate roots she had been searching for:

> It was by chance that I came to live in this village. I have lived
> most of my life in shattered little bits. Somehow, here, the
> shattered bits began to grow together. There is a sense of
> woverness, a wholeness in life here, a feeling of how strange and
> beautiful people can be - just living. People do much subsistence
> living here, and so much mud living; for Serowe is, on the
> whole, a sprawling village of mud huts. (Serowe X)

Serowe in its semi documentary forms afforded Head the opportunity to
complete the gathering of the treasures which her novels and short stories are an
important part of. This is why inspite of her ethnographic posture the same lyric
beauty with which she wrote of the Botswana land and people colours these
personal accounts from people of different ages and occupations. It is still a
celebration of the distinctive life of these villagers:

> Mixing historical commentary of her own with recorded
> statements and comments from the villagers themselves, she
> creates an affectionate picture of an isolated community gradually
> changing under a series of benign autocrats and a typically free
> from extensive white settlement or influence. (p.8).

With the narrative space between speakers and readers collapsed, the
elders, craftsmen and women of Serowe relate to us in their words , in their
own idioms the events of the historical period starting with the benevolent
despotism of Khama the Great (1875-1923) and his successor Tshekedi Khama

(1926-59) and bringing the history of the village up-to-date by way of Patrick Van Rensburg's Swaneng Project (1963). It is the history of Gohema Mmidi and Motabeng rewritten with unusual immediacy.

In her introduction, among other things Head explains to us the value of names as landmarks; they evoke stories of events which took place at the time of people's birth, a practice shared by many African societies. But in the context of Head's works names become doubly significant. "So, no one has a meaningless name and often the word combinations that make up a person's name are quite new and original," says Head. (XXII). Naming is a means towards the individuation of character, and to a novelist who placed such a premium on the uniqueness of the individual names automatically underscore what is special in each character and personality. It gives him an identity. But Serowe is more about the people as a whole than about individuals, with the exception of the three leaders who with their ideas and ideals contributed most to the transformation of Serowe. Her abiding portrait of Serowe is that of an industrious people. Head claims the Serowans have never lacked direction, but have always been involved in causes and debates; that no other village in Botswana is as dynamic as Serowe, that they have always had leadership in their midst and tended to identify genius with traditional leadership. Comparing Serowe with other towns she writes:

> But the construction of Serowe intimately involved its population. They always seem to be building Serowe with their bare hands and little tools - a hoe, an axe and mud - that's all. This intimate knowledge of construction covers every aspect of village life. Each member of the community is known; his latest scandal, his latest love affair. (p XII).

The voices we hear are therefore no more than representative individuals through whom the writer intended to leave us with verbal records of the old craft methods such as ploughing, potting, basket making, tanning thatching; the preacher, teacher, thatcher and market woman - these people and skills are part and parcel of the story of Serowe. By so doing she assumed the ancient responsibility of great chronicler, and historian, philosopher - queen and martyr (witness).

Ella Robinson has said that Head's world is a world of thought and of books. (Robinson 1990) but she also quickly adds that the people, the earth and all living things are an integral part of that world. People are always at the centre of Head's vision; they are the makers and unmakers of society; the creators and destroyers of happiness and justice. Despite the countless topics covered in <u>Serowe</u>, such as war, politics, traditional religion and Christianity, medicine, traditional and western, farming and other forms of occupations, creative and technical; family life, love and the laws that govern these, it is the people who practised those that live in the reader's imagination after the text has been put down. Head follows this vision, and uses this human-centred approach in her novels, short stories and ethnographic accounts of the people and village of Serowe.

CHAPTER 6

A NICHE FOR BESSIE HEAD

In his critical work, <u>Myth, Literature and the African World</u> (1976), Wole Soyinka criticised Western Theatre, producers and audiences for their failure when confronted with African ritual drama, or drama of the gods; and blamed them for interpretations and presentations which have been largely responsible for a multitude of false concepts. Soyinka saw this shortcoming as the consequence of the Western European man's fondness for reducing essences into specialist terminologies through a chronic habit of compartmentalization. These comments apply to other literary discourses; as Soyinka also says:

> It is by the way a very catching habit; we have all caught it to some extent.[1]

Literary critics are familiar with these endless compartments, categories and neatly formulated theories in jealously guarded critical spaces, and the structures of perception which they impose on writers and texts. More and more works are approached from rigid individualistic, isolationist and authoritative camps built on conditioned and limited interests and prejudices; and creativity is now judged rather than assessed through synthesis, evaluation and contextuality. Oppositional discursive strategies easily take the form of attacks, dismissals and rejections of conflicting approaches, to the exclusion of equally valuable critical

---

[1] Wole Soyinka. <u>Myth, Literature nd the African World.</u> Cambridge: Cambridge University Press, 1990, p.6.

positions and modes of exploration. Such critical postures and attitudes ultimately deny competing regimes of truth, experience and interpretation, and by implication the fluid nature of writing and critical evaluation of the written text.

Critical pontification by its very nature is devoid of respect for different approaches to literature. It also belies some form of prescription which some writers find more difficult than others to accept. Bessie Head's disavowal of feminism perhaps was a form of protest against such partisan dogmatism which ignores the intricacies, manifestations, faces and natures of women's oppression in the individual, national and international contexts. Her protest therefore constitutes a form of ideology intended to emphasize the recognition of such delicate intersections in gender issues.

In South Africa apartheid has for centuries been the thematic focus of creativity and critical discourse and has provided a unique platform for self-expression. It touches everyone and everything. In Jacques Berthoud's words:

> What singles out apartheid is its attempt to subject the whole range of human interests--material, social, cultural--to the intrinsic meaninglessness of colour difference. It is the project of organising the ongoing life of a nation (not of dispatching a segment of it into the vacuum of the final solution) on the basis of a purely artificial principle, or more accurately of a superstition--that is, a belief originating only in the fantasies of its adherents.[2]

The binary oppositional imperative in this statement is race, a reality which permeates or poisons areas of human interaction so subtly or so overtly that it remains permanently inscribed on every author's mind. Even without any deliberate act of historicisation, the sympathetic critic can find excuses for Nadine Gordimer's similar rejection of women's issues in the early 1980s, for she considered feminism less serious and severe than the hydra-headed nuances and repercussions of Apartheid which tramples so blindly and brutally on human rights. Yet the complexities and irony of her posture prove that she understands that gender   is often a strong social determinant inextricable from its racial

---

[2] Jacques Berthoud "Writing under Apartheid," Current Writing Text and Reception in South Africa. Vol. 1, No. 1, October 1989, p.78.

source, and is sometimes more multi-sided than is immediately apparent. Nevertheless Head is not Gordimer, and in spite of her much heralded disavowal of feminism she is vital to the development of a woman-centred discourse committed to unravelling the silences of women through a creative style which has focused attention on their oppression by a male-dominated society in the past and the present.

Bessie Head's position in the ongoing debate over the relationship between writing and the overall struggle of South Africa for social, political, racial and sexist liberation, has for long been a source of concern to fellow writers--male and female; Lewis Nkosi's complaint about her lack of overt political commitment being a case in point. Comparing Mphahlde and Bessie Head Nkosi writes:

> Significantly, in A Question of Power, a novel in which the autobiographical element holds an intolerable sway over the novelist, the mental breakdown of the heroine is accompanied by a parallel breakdown in communication, with an increasing loss of this power to instruct or arouse sympathy, which is only intermittently relieved by periodic flashes of intense illumination.
>
> Sooner or later we have to come back to the question of 'protest' and 'commitment' which looms so large whenever South African fiction is discussed. Bessie Head is not a political novelist in any sense we can recognise; indeed, there is ample evidence that she is generally hostile to politics. Far from being an axiomatic proposition, as some critics with an innate hostility to politics tend to believe, this lack of precise political commitment weakens rather than aids Bessie Head's grasp of character.[3]

The irony of Nkosi's position is that it simply demonstrates his inability to appreciate this aspect of Head's work because of his own ideological expectations and mode of exploration. Writing, especially in South Africa, is a political act, but the legislation of the mode of inscribing issues in texts can only efface the distinguishing qualities of each individual writer, which is essential for a people just emerging from a long history of silence. Mbulelo Mzamane's

---

[3] Lewis Nkosi, Tasks and Masks: Themes and Styles of African Literature U.K. Longmans 1981, p.102.

contribution to the Volume I of <u>Current Writing</u> takes up this question with all
its political, cultural and literary implications:

> Few people in the world today feel the need more acutely than
> the disadvantaged and oppressed people of South Africa to define
> and explain themselves to the world, to strip their image of the
> insults that have been hurled at it, and to arrest the further
> erosion of their culture and humanity by the "dominant" and
> largely superimposed culture in their land.[4]

Mbulelo is willing to accept revisionism, mythification and
romanticisation as valid formalistic modes in this task. Zoë Wicomb has
attempted to subject <u>Maru</u> to theoretical and critical strategies which foreground
irony as Head's creative hallmark:

> I have not justified my use of postmodernist theory; there is no
> room to deal with the many and diverse issues raised by
> "Feminism(s) and Writing in South Africa". But I can think of
> no more useful an approach which would allow us for instance to
> re-read Bessie Head, not in terms of her avowed anti-feminism,
> but in terms of the issues in her discourse where illegitimate
> meanings percolate through and so undermine an overt womanist
> message.[5]

The emphasis falls on the validity of a multiplicity of reading levels and
interpretations which Wicomb posits as a desirable paradigm:

> A possible approach then to South African women's writing
> would be to examine discursive strategies by which the orthodox
> tendency or hierarchising the evils of our society--racism,
> sexism, classism--is resisted, or the ways in which the conflicting
> demands of representing these are textually articulated.[6]

---

[4] Mzamane, Mbulelo. "An Unhistoric Will into the Past" <u>Current Writing</u>, Vol, Vol-1, No. 1,
October 1989. p.36.

[5] Ibid., p.43

[6] Op.cit., p.42.

Head's total literary achievement is ripe for another critical examination which would take the form of a tribute to her works and life, one close to that undertaken in The Tragic Life (Abrahams, 1988); Critical discourse has sufficiently inscribed her talent under the autobiography, the utopia, quiet protest and feminism separately. But more and more her genius seems to defy such conventional literary labelling.

Bessie Head's works provide a compendium of themes and forms already attempted by various African writers, but now stamped with her very original vision in a style marked by intensity and profundity. Her talent can be approached from various angles, all equally valid. She is an accomplished story-teller, the sensitive chronicler of the sights and sounds of rural Botswana, and its people's hopes and dreams. She is both a champion of the cause of women and at the same time a critic of their passivity and acquiescence in the face of oppression. No writer has written so personally, so passionately and yet so universally about the painful experience of exile; its excruciating physical and emotional loneliness which in her special case were further complicated by the sexual dimensions of being a woman, with their attendant powerlessness, voicelessness and helplessness. But apartheid in her context has always been less a matter of racial segregation and discrimination against black South Africans by their white compatriots, and more of any group discriminating against another on grounds of race, sex or physical characteristics such as the Masarwa alone understand. Head insisted on perceiving these problems as universal ones without ignoring the particular circumstances of South Africa and Botswana. In carving out a niche for her, critics must resist the temptation to relegate her to the narrow group of feminist, utopian or protest writers. Her imagination, experience and art were too grounded on the earth and too informed by common sense to belong comfortably to any of these groups. She is a complex writer, and her assessment must therefore not be reduced to a pattern of themes, because even in handling her special themes each was perceived not just as social or historical incidents but as timeless aspects of the human mind. She has an insistent manner which makes her characters and events eternal paradigms.

Head also knew the pain of identity crisis more deeply than most people. Kiersten Holst Peterson identifies what is peculiar to Head's experience of identity crisis:

She is a coloured South African, and the story of her origin is
that her white mother conceived her with a black stable boy. She
was insane, or rather her society thought that this act was proof
of insanity, so she was put in a mental hospital, where she
eventually committed suicide. Meanwhile her child, Bessie Head,
was brought up in a series of child care institutions and foster
homes, and she eventually left South Africa as a political refugee
to end up as a stateless person in Botswana. This life story
constitutes the ultimate in alienation. Bessie Head does not
literally know who she is. . . . [7]

Identity crisis was one of the earliest themes explored by African male
writers. An aspect of the cultural nationalism of the nineteen fifties was the
examination of what colonialism did to the identity of the African personality
who was caught between two cultures, both of which he no longer could fully
identify with. The search for roots which dominates Head's works therefore has
a living equivalent in Achebe's and Ngugi's works. In experience and literary
inscription, however, Head's representations although mostly autobiographical,
surpass their East and West African counterparts in intensity:

I could say that I have the stamina to survive the sort of situations
only wild alley cats encounter, but I would not like to take on
another birth in South Africa and end up in Botswana.
...No one cares. Why the hell did you come here in the first
place, they say? We don't want you. And behind you is such hell
and calamity that one simply asks: Oh God why was I born?
What other effort do I make to survive? Where do I go. Or on
which day do I die?[8]

Certainly no where else in African literature, East, South or West has
the agony of identity crisis been articulated in such painful and desperate terms.
Rootlessness is at the heart of the speaker's cry and only in literature of the
diaspora can a reader spy a near equivalent.

---

[7] Paterson, Kierston. "Unpopular Opinions. Some African Women Writers." Kunapipi, P. 120.

[8] Bryce, Jane. "In Remembrance of Bessie Head." The Guardian Sunday Supplement, July 27,
1986 P. B4

The theme of madness is an extension of the foregoing. African authors have generally been unsuccessful in representing madness. The case of Chinua Achebe's Ezeulu is one of the most convincing especially when compared with that of Kofo Awoonor's Amamu, where madness becomes an escape valve from societal pressures for a morally and psychologically weak hero incapable of confronting them. In Head's, A Question of Power, madness becomes a special aspect of exile-writing which has always been a distinct category of South African writing, and by the same token carries the responsibility of having to meet certain expectations in theme and style, such as one finds in the poetry of Dennis Brutus and Arthur Nortje. Head lacked the strong racial identity which constitutes the mainstay of most black South Africans under an inhuman and oppressive regime. Ironically South Africa remained the only cultural background available to her as a point of reference. In and out of South Africa she was an outsider and the accompanying experience eventually caused her retreat into madness. It is the result of her failure to establish some form of identity, however tenuous anywhere; for with all her love for the land of Botswana, it remained for her a site of contradictions where she was always considered an oddity.

In A Question of Power Elizabeth's nightmarish and obscene encounters become the imaginative expression of Head's life of abuse and her private suffering among the Botswana, and by extension the sufferings of all the despised, rejected and oppressed in human history. The process of Elizabeth's mental breakdown, her hallucinatory sessions, her restless nights of torture, and screaming from the monsters that torment her can only be so accurately and so intensely created perhaps, as Arthur Ravenscroft says, only "by a novelist who had herself gone through similar experience." In assessing her particular achievement in this regard, the critic must marvel at such perfect fusion of subject and object, and the calibre and stature of a creative imagination which is capable of maintaining such a clear separation of identity between Elizabeth the fictive character and Bessie Head the novelist. Head literally dramatises for the audience the process of what Ravenscroft appropriately calls her 'epic purgatory' captured without sentimentality and without self pity, in order that the reader may better appreciate the resemblance between private insanity and the insanity of deranged societies all over the world. Head was born into madness, lived it and recreated it in literature with the intensity, familiarity and understanding of a victim, and the confidence of an assured artist.

Although the theme of apartheid colours almost every page of Bessie Head's novels she refuses to limit its connotation to the hackneyed political one of white versus black. What one finds in her works is a personal approach which compares the internal and external possibilities of such a power system:

> To her apartheid is not different from tribal racism: the oppression of black by white is equal to the oppression of women by social systems which gives inordinate prestige and power to men.[9]

She also undertook representations of tribal politics, but her treatment is a far cry from Achebe's treatment of the sectional interest and petty jealousies of Ezeulu, the chief priest and his colleagues in Arrow of God: it embraces the issue of power from a personal, particular point of view and moves to a general and sustained exploration of the fundamental questions of racial and social identity, the nature of all power "and the parallel struggles of the individual for self-realisation, and people for social transformation." Head knew racial, social and sexual oppression. Born into alienation it is understandable that she should visualise a future world, a future African society where today's injustices and inequalities will no more exist. Tribal injustices constitute a major part of her humiliating circumstances of suffering. She looks at the society with its internal contradictions for what they are. African literature has broached the question of corruption in the political system of the town and city but has shied away from its parallel in the tribal or village structure.

But Head takes the tribalist aspect of traditional Botswana society through her usual permutations. She portrays it as a corrupt and exploitative system in which irresponsible chiefs live off the slave labour of their subjects. It retards progress and oppresses and abuses women who most of the time remain docile and dull. The escapades of chief Matenge and Sekoto his brother in When Rain Clouds Gather are well-known; so is the sexual ruthlessness of Moleka in

---

[9] Jane Bryce. "In Remembrance of Bessie Head" The Guardian Sunday Supplement July 27, 1986. P. B4.

Maru. The chiefs are characteristically supported by a gang of new self-seeking politicians. Matenge is greedy, nasty in personality and over-bearing. He is a terror to his own people, and accordingly loses his life in the attempt to humiliate Paulina Sobeso, having previously failed to intimidate Gilbert and get Makhaya deported.

Chinua Achebe's introduction and tactful handling of social and political apartheid against the Osus of Iboland, in No Longer at Ease (1960) is the closest attempt by an African author to face the full ugliness of tribal and ethnic apartheid. The case of the Masarwa in Maru stands out in bold relief in its obvious irony. A critic has put it very philosophically:

> The irony in the context of Botswana, vis-a-vis the problem of race subsists in the fact that the black races who are at the receiving end of the white man's iniquitous philosophy of race relations, are themselves the practitioners of similar policies towards the Masarwa. Perhaps the evil in man must necessarily find an outlet in racial discrimination because as it appears there doesn't exist a single nation which is free of this propensity.[10]

It takes a political voice to call attention to the slavery of these untouchables whose sub human status is a given in a society totally blind to the internal weaknesses within its political and social arrangement. The elder Margaret Cadmore confesses her inability to understand the "beastliness" of society to the Masarwa. Unlike the Osus of Iboland, the Masarwa were betrayed by physical characteristics, and in addition lacked the educational privilege and material security enjoyed by the former. Unlike women and blacks, they were not marginalised; they did not exist on the edges of society with diminished nights. They rather skirted fearfully on the fringes of a clearly hostile and cruel community--as slaves occasionally treated "nicely" by their owners. Their position erases the problematics of sexism, or classism and reinstitutes the ultimate question of racism, which is humanism:

> In Botswana they say: Zebras, Lions, Buffalo and Bushmen live
> in the Kalahari Desert. If you can catch a Zebra, you can walk up

---

[10] Rukmini Vanamali, A Question of Violence. Maru "A Question of Power," Unpublished paper, University of Calabar, 1983, p. 6.

to it, forcefully open its mouth and examine its teeth. The Zebra
is not supposed to mind because it is an animal. Scientists do the
same to Bushmen and they are not supposed to mind because
there is no one they can still turn around to and say `At least I
am not a --' of all things that are said of oppressed people, the
worst things are said and done to the Bushmen. Ask the
scientists. Haven't they yet written a treatise on how Bushmen
are an oddity of the human race, who are half the head of a man
and half the body of a donkey? (Head, 11)

Bessie Head is the voice, the primary and essential witness, speaking,
writing, teaching and helping to foster alternative action through language. The
text therefore is her political strategy, and Maru's, Dikeledi's and Moleka's
cultural revaluation in the treatment of their slaves and their sense of
professional responsibility are necessary first steps.

For the psychological agony of the sufferer Head has this to say:

...What was a Bushman supposed to do? She had no weapons of
words or personality, only a permanent silence and a face which
revealed no emotion, except that now and then an abrupt tear
would splash down out of one eye.[11]

The commotion caused in Dilepe School at the discovery of Margaret's
true race by her colleagues borders on farce, but her foster-mother had told her,
"environment is everything, heredity nothing." And so armed with that
philosophy, and a resilient character remarkable for its patience, maturity of
vision and adaptability she survives the gibes, the taunts, the assaults and insults
of "the vicious, the selfish, the cruel, "those noted for their capacity to create
misery; and wakes up one morning in a little house surrounded by yellow
daisies to look back at that year as "the most vital and vivid of her life."

If Head exposes the habits and prejudices of Botswana she also watched
her women labour as home-keepers, mothers, workers and sexual tools of men.
Exploited and oppressed they have evolved a way of life in which they expected
very little from their men. Head vouches for them without reservation:

---

[11] Bessie Head. Maru London. Ibadan, Nairobi: Heinemann, 1971, p.12. Further references to
the text can be found in the essay.

> It was always like this. Any little thing was an adventure. They
> were capable of pitching themselves into the hardest, most
> sustained labour with perhaps the same joy that society women in
> other parts of the world experience when they organise fetes or
> tea parties. No men ever worked harder than Botswana women,
> for the whole burden of providing food for big families rested
> with them. It was their sticks that thrashed the corn at harvesting
> time and their winnowing baskets that filled the air for miles and
> miles around with the dust of husks, and they often, in addition
> to broadcasting the seed when the early rains fell, took over the
> tasks of the men and also ploughed the land with oxen.[12]

This feminist representation rejects the usual dwelling on marriage and motherhood for an exploration of the "more profound terms of power relationships where the key to a betterment of women's position, which she desires and advocates, lies in keeping the power-hungry systems, personalities and aspects of one's character in check. Head understood their predicament: surrounded by men who believe that their roving occupation as wandering cattle rearers automatically absolves them from fulfilling their roles as farmers in a basically agricultural society, the women have plunged themselves body and spirit into the agricultural life and activities of the society. And faced with a situation where their men have never appreciated the romantic treasurings of love, they have likewise learnt to perfectly suppress all that is romantic in their relationships with men. Head highlights their adaptability in the face of physical and emotional deprivation, economic and sexual abuse; their survival strategy.

The agricultural projects at Golema Mmidi and Motabeng are regenerative spaces of intense creativity and productivity, and a haven for the lost and the lonely of different societies. They also show Head's women at their best. They people that world of everyday reality, the ordinary, the very mundane on which Head was able to anchor even Elizabeth's worst hallucinations. They have grace, resilience and strength. Isabelle Matsikidze, in analysing what she calls Head's "redemptive political philosophy", calls attention to her positive representation of women in her writing:

---

[12] When Rain Clouds Gather London: Heinemann 1968, p. 104 Further references can be found in the essay.

In all these claims about the South African situation, what
remains most intriguing to me is the position of Head's women.
Dikeledi, for example, does not remain in the kitchen. Her roles
are not tied to her female biology alone. She is wife and mother
and also an intellectual and leader, just as Moleka will be a
husband, father, and also a leader. Women's perceptions are not
radically different from those of their male counterparts...The
image of women in Maru comes through only as they play their
part in society not below men, not above them, or separate from
them, but side by side with them, each gender equally affecting
the political tone of society. (p.108)

Besides the role of women, she was equally interested in a "new world
of compassion, justice and goodness which in a way makes her a utopian writer.
In this context her distinguishing quality is that she wrote with hope. She was
also a utopian writer with a difference. She visualised a special society
recommended, by both a revolutionary agricultural challenge of taming a semi-
arid desert, and a moral utopia which nevertheless takes cognizance of all
possible threats, human and otherwise. She has no room for the African writer's
nostalgia for the past. Head's world is all man-made. It has no room for the
petty squabbles and caprices of unseen powers whose intervention too often
poisons human relationships and retards progress. Her powerful and tough
imagination functions for the future. Apart from stamping Botswana, its history,
political structure, tribal norms and prejudices on the literary map of Africa she
has also x-rayed the shortcomings of that structure and criticised tribal racism.
She was the underdog among underdogs, but refused to stay under; born a
victim but lived as a survivor. In a world typified by obscene lust for power,
monumental injustice and oppression of the weak, she did not recommend
abstention from action, but rather modest action in very practical terms, with
individual hearts flushed and cleansed of collective purpose. As Ravenscroft
says, "The divinity she acknowledges is a new less arrogant kind of humanism,
a remorseless God who demands that iron integrity in personal conduct should
inform political action too".[13] Although she allows her male characters to
choose between despotic and benevolent power, Head invests in all men and

---

13 Arthur Ravenscript. "The Novels of Bessie Head" Aspects of South African Literature.
Christopher Heywood (Ed) London, Ibadan Nairobi, Lusaka: Heinemann, 1976, p.185.

women the power to contribute towards the realisation of this humane world. It may not be, like Maru's and Margaret's home, a place "thousand miles away where the sun rose, new and new each day" (p.125). But it promises to be certainly better than the world Head knew, and by inference, the world we all know.

An appreciation of Head's contribution to African literary discourse must start with an understanding that though she was not fully an African by ancestry, she saw herself as one, and struggled to be one. Though she lost that battle of identity she lived and wrote of the much sung African spirit of brotherhood and love of communal life as no other African author did. Head loved Africa, its land and its people, though psychologically she lived and died at the edge of that society, considered strange and eccentric by her fellow Botswanans. This fundamental contradiction explains why in all her novels especially A Question of Power, any temptation towards romantic idealisation is promptly undercut by a timely recourse to humour, pathos or outright sarcasm. In Jane Bryce's words:

> ...As the mood dips and soars between the abyss and ecstasy, the
> style too juxtaposes extreme mundanity and lyricism. (p.84)

"The reiterated affirmatives in Bessie Head's discourse are the 'dignity', the 'peacefulness', the 'courtesies', the 'goodness' represented by rural Botswana" (Mackenzie, p.167). In her inscription of those qualities, recovery and growth follow upon alienation and exile just as her personal story is "a career of eloquent and poignant symmetry, pivoting upon, and ultimately dedicated to the hallowed ground of Serowe" (p.167). In it the objects and receivers of oppression and horror; the victims of abuse, the outcasts of society; the playthings of men; the eternal shadows locked in eternal silence acquire an alternative space, a community life of self-definition where their silence is transformed into language and action because her dream of an ideal Africa was always threatened by the fear of its non-realizability.

Serowe is a miniature of her larger new world, but even in that near utopian context she did not fail to highlight the horror of the darker aspects of African traditions and cherished customs which continue to violate individual lives.

She encapsulated all these factors in her works--she touched the old familiar themes of African literature but in doing so refused to take refuge in the established but very delimiting categories. She had a deep, intense and expansive imagination which gave profundity to hackneyed topics. She also wrote on what Kiersten Holst Peterson called "unpopular opinions" on tribal politics, power, love and sex. Her mythology of the future is all her own, anchored in an earth-bound pragmatism. Her imagination was perhaps most alive in the passages of lyrical tenderness devoted to the praise of the everyday, and which crystallize her special love for Africa. Of that love Bryce writes, citing Head's comments on A Question of Power:

> I might like to say that I made a gesture towards Africa, captured the national statement of its soul, that soul deeply sinks into my own soul, that I might for centuries have been working on the ideal of the equality of man and found that only African people have it built into their social structure in a perfected form. (p.B4)

Like Jane Bryce we all hope that if this belief could not save her life, it at least saved her soul. All aspects of her large soul, tough imaginative and arresting style must be taken into consideration in assessing her achievement as a literary marvel, and one not afraid to advance her moral idealism in a world which now scoffs at such. She was more than just a feminist, protest, utopian or autobiographical writer.

She was all these put together, as well as the most potent and compelling female voice in the tradition. Only a niche special enough to accommodate all these discursive and philosophical achievements can we justifiably carve out for her in the African literary hall of fame.

CHAPTER 7

CONCLUSION

Flora Nwapa, Buchi Emecheta and Bessie Head
The Question of Authenticity

The twentieth century is the age of literary criticism and critical theory, a period characterised by a remarkable proliferation of theories investigating the meaning of literature, reading and criticism, sometimes so abstractly, scientifically, and mechanically executed that the original humanistic foundation of literature is lost in the context of opposing theories and clashing critical jargons. But theory or its excesses, has its friends as well as its foes. Abiola Irele once wrote in reference to this phenomenon:

> Literary criticism has been moved beyond, in something of a forced march, into such diverse territories as psychoanalysis, Russian Formalism, Phenomenology, Structuralism and Semiotics, and more recently, "Deconstruction". There is now such a proliferation of theories and of schools that the discipline can no longer be said to have a fixed centre of canons and procedures. When this happens to an academic discipline, we can be sure there is something amiss![1]

---

[1] Abiola Irele, "Literary Criticism in the Nigerian Context", in <u>Perspectives on Nigerian Literature 1700 to the Present</u>. Vol 1 Nigeria: Guardian Literary Series, 1988, p.94.

Although Feminism is one of such theories; in its case struggling to form a theoretical base for the validation of a female oriented literature, and for the evaluation of other forms of imaginative expression, Feminist scholars are also very suspicious of the more dogmatic theories like Structuralism. Raman Seldon offers a personal explanation for this suspicion by the advocates of Feminism:

> There are many reasons for this. In academic institutions 'theory' is often male, even macho; it is hard, intellectual avant-garde of literary studies. The manly virtues of rigour thrusting purpose, and rampant ambition find their home in theory rather than in the often tender art of critical interpretation.[2]

Seldon further claims that much Feminist criticism wishes to escape the "fixities" and "definites" of theory and to develop a female discourse which cannot be tied down conceptually as belonging to a recognised and therefore male-produced, theoretical tradition. Since Seldon does not support his claims statistically or posit them as absolute truths, an interested critic can therefore extract what suits his or her purposes. He is however correct when he states that "Feminist criticism sometimes summons up the anger of the Furies in order to disturb the complacent certainties of patriarchal culture and to create a less oppressive climate for women writers and readers." (Seldon 128). Feminism like most movements, does have its excesses, but it is more about positives than negatives. In its long and arduous journey it has passed the stage of simple repudiation of previous formulations about women; from a radical perspective about literature and sex roles to a tentative beginning in the development of a feminist literary aesthetic.[3] This aesthetic embraces the analytical and interpretative, the contextual and non-contextual. It insists on reassessment, and by that act has added to the corpus of critical material on many works dealing with women. Josephine Donovan once called its method an "excavational" one which in its flexibility also considers the polemical, the political and

---

[2] Raman Seldon. A Reader's Guide to Contemporary Literary Theory. Lexington, Kentucky: The University Press of Kentucky, 1958, p.129.

[3] See Josephine Donovan (ed.) Feminist Literary Criticism, Explorations in Theory. Lexington: The University Press of Kentucky, for more isight into Feminist approaches to criticism.

sociological as well as the humanistic and ethical in contrast to the exclusivist and closed approaches of Deconstruction and Structuralism. It is also cross-cultural and analogic. This comprehensive attitude is also important for the consideration of African Women writers in the context of Feminism in African literature which this chapter undertakes.

The emergence of African literature started much later than the history of Feminist consciousness in African Societies. For a long time however African literature remained the preserve of men until Ama Ata Aidoo, Flora Nwapa, Grace Ogot, Adaora Ulasi and Bessie Head came into the literary scene from around 1966. This imbalance was due to several factors. First the Colonial institutions chose men for formal education while women were prepared for family life and marriage. Traditional attitudes, worked out within the family, also collided with Colonialism to deny women the benefits of formal education and consequently of the benefits of literary creativity. But from the nineteen seventies, and especially in the eighties African women writers have increased in such numbers that criticism has also responded to the development. The rise has also resulted in the recent emphasis on women writers who now form the cornerstone of what can be regarded as African Feminist Aesthetics. Although it has much in common with its Western counterpart it also differs in other fundamental ways, in themes, approaches and perspectives.

Criticism has amply and exhaustively examined the dominant themes which engaged the interest of African women writers, their language, characterisation and imagery; and occasionally employing a methodology which compares such feminist output with those of male criticism in order to point out areas of misrepresentation and stereotyping women's lives and needs by male writers. Lloyd Brown's work Women Writers of Black Africa (1981) is the first exhaustive critical study on these writers; and while it highlights their thematic and stylistic achievements, Brown does not fail to point out the shortcomings in other areas. Carole Boyce Davies has enumerated the major concerns of African women writers as:

> 1) motherhood (the presence or absence of it/its joys and pains: 2) the vagaries of living in a polygamous marriage: 3) the oppression of colonialism and white rule: 4) the struggle for economic independence: 5) the achievement of a balance between

relationships with men and friendships with other women: 6) the
fickleness of husbands: 7) the importance of having a support
system, particularly in the urban environment: 8) the mother-
daughter conflict or relationship: 9) the mother-son relationship;
10) above all, the definition of self or the development of a
separate self over and beyond, but not separate from tradition or
other man-made restrictions.[4]

I wish to re-examine the treatment of those issues by women writers; to
revisit the issue of female stereotypes and images by Feminist writers, and to
isolate signs and factors which militate against a more liberating imaginative
vision in some of their works. The prestigious journal African Literature Today
declared its acknowledgement of the literary effort of African women writers by
devoting its fifteenth issue to women writers and the presentation of women in
African Literature. That this editorial gesture should take place as recently as
1987 is disappointing, although it remains one of the first in the history of
African Literary Journals. The Griot also devoted its 1987 Summer Edition to
Gender Issues. These journals were published six years after Lloyd Brown
published Women Writers in Black Africa (1981); two years after Oladele
Taiwo published Women Novelists in Modern Africa (1984) and two years after
Brenda Barrian and Mildred Mortimer sent to Africa World Press their
collection, Critical Perspectives on Women Writers from Africa (1985). All
these works together with a large body of minor books, journal articles and
anthologies give ample evidence that the neglect of these writers by critics is no
longer an issue. Perhaps Flora Nwapa and Buchi Emecheta and Bessie Head as
the three most prolific of the group have received most attention. Their works
are the storehouse of the experience, history, wisdom, culture of women; they
should be the most authentic voices and exponents of women's social, economic
and political roles in society; they are the mouthpiece of millions of women who
have lived and continue to live under various forms of oppression and
deprivation, and mostly lacking a voice to remedy their powerlessness or even
the capacity to understand it. They are witnesses to their years of abuse and

---

[4] Carole Bryce Davies - "Introduction: Feminist Consciousness and African Literary Criticism"
in Ngambika: Studies of Women in African Literature Trenton, New Jersey: Africa World
Press, Inc., 1986, ed. by Carole Boyce Davies and Anne Adams Graves.

neglect. These roles have been critically examined in many journals.

The first article in the above-mentioned issue of ALT no. 15, by Omolara Ogundipe-Leslie heralds a new attitude and a very desirable and healthy one to the works of these writers. She has resurrected the nearly dead horse of commitment in African literary criticism, but this time with reference to African women writers.[5] While I may disagree with her prescriptive approach which outlines themes that must be treated by such writers, I do agree with her more fundamental insistence on the responsibility of the writer to the reader especially within the context of a realistic novel which presupposes a universe of shared experience--historical, cultural; emotional and psychological--between the writer and her readership. Although Flora Nwapa and Buchi Emecheta are well known for saying they are not Feminist writers, they require a total departure in their thematic concerns to convince critics of that fact. For the purposes of this chapter it is sufficient that they have written about African women in different situations and at different historical periods.

Reading is a shared relationship and therefore authorises the reader to judge works by the "truth criterion" as expounded by Marcia Holly in Feminine Literary Criticism. She asks:

> Is it necessary, then, to know a writer's background in order to criticise her/his work? Yes and no. To determine whether or not a person has written in bad faith, we must indeed know about her/his life. But to determine its psychological authenticity we need only have the work and an unbiased understanding of human needs, motivations and emotions. But positions require movement away from Formalist criticism and insist that we judge by standards of authenticity.[6]

African women writers are the representatives of the other voice, the chroniclers of the nature, character and destiny of African women, traditional

---

[5] Omolara Ogundipe-Leslie. "The Female Writer and her Commitment" African Literature Today, no. 15, (ed) Eldred D. Jones: London: James Currey Ltd., 1987, pp.51-13.

[6] Marcia Holly "Consciousness and Authenticity: Toward a Feminist Aesthetic" in Feminist Literary Criticism (ed.) Josephine Donovan. Lexington: The University Press of Kentucky, 1989, pp. 38-47.

and modern; and such an onerous task is bound to attract a wealth of critical reactions. I therefore consider this exercise part of the ongoing critical dialogue on works of three of these writers, Flora Nwapa, Buchi Emecheta and Bessie Head; and adopt an attitude which assumes that texts are by human authors for human readers about human subjects, to borrow from the theory of humanistic formalism advanced by Daniel Schwarz: It is a theory that confidently questions the nature of the voice speaking to us in a literary work and does not fear to probe the attitudes, beliefs, values and feelings of the writer while taking into account the form, structure, mode of narrative, patterns of language, diction, rhythm and meaning as opposed to the totalitarian method and dogma of Formalism which insists on one and only one way of reading a text. Georg Lukacs once wrote:

> Humanism, that is, the passionate study of man's nature, is essential to all literature and art; and good art and good literature are humanistic to the extent that they not only investigate man and the real essence of his nature with passion but also and simultaneously defend human integrity passionately against all attacks, degradation and distortion.[7]

Whether this be the exploitation of man by man, man by women, woman by man or the rich by the poor, the statement remains a significant critical pronouncement which assumes more urgency in Postcolonial, Third World and Feminist Literature. In differentiating between naturalistic art and real art, the latter is identified as representing life in "its totality, in motion, development and evolution". The sex of characters ought not to control the humaneness of their conflict or response. Women writers in Africa, especially, Nwapa and Emecheta often present facile answers and invalid personal solutions to complex social questions and as a result have fallen into the sexual stereotyping of women which male writers have been accused of. African literary criticism, especially Feminist criticism must not shy away from this problem. The question is: How authentic are the images of women presented in their works? Is it not true that male writers have up till now presented more convincing

---

[7] Ibid; p.47; "Georg Lukacs' Writer and Critic" cited in Marcia Holly's article.

images of African women in literature.?[8] It is one thing to aim for characters that stimulate empathetic identification in the readers and illustrate the depths which women's sufferings can attain; it is however another thing to assault the reader's intelligence by presenting an unending string of women like Nnu Ego of The Joys of Motherhood whose lives are totally out of tune with historical realities. There are too many of what Carole Boyce Davies calls the invisible, mute, voiceless woman who exists only as tangential to men and their problems. Ten years to the end of the twentieth century the image of the African woman in novels written by women is that of the eternal and unchanging victim, victimised by church, by family, by husband, by tradition and incapable of making any permanent or convincing gesture towards self-fulfilment or protest. When she aspires to self assertion, this significant act is affirmed with a proscribed metaphor, within which like a bird in a spacious cage, she is allowed so much space and no more. Eventually she settles down, having fluttered powerless wings within her confined space. Invariably the conflict takes place within marriage. In it she is condemned to try and fail; and whenever she dares break away she metamorphoses into a whore. Most of the works end on an indecisive note and a confused destiny for the heroine. In her inability to handle this recurrent lack of subtlety and ambiguousness, Catherine Frank writes, with particular reference to Buchi Emecheta's Double Yoke:

> It is a strange but perhaps realistic conclusion...Double Yoke, in short, poses a problem rather than providing a solution. But despite the uncertainty of its conclusion, it clearly demonstrates that women and men in contemporary African society are at war with one another, that women cannot hope to vanquish their oppressors in open combat. Instead, they must cleverly exploit their exploiters and their retreat for their emotional needs to a separate world of women.[9]

Significantly the title of the article is "Women without Men: The Feminist novel in Africa" in which she also sadly enthrones Debbie Ogedemgbe

[8] This statement is relevant to Isidore Okpewho, Ngugi Wa Thiong'o Ousmane Sembere and Chinua Achebe.

[9] Buchi Emecheta. Double Yoke. London: Ogwugwu Afor Company, 1982, p.24.

of Destination Biafra (1982) as the apotheosis of the African New Woman. That such a flat character, an obvious stereotype, predictable and undeveloped should become a critic's model, attests to the dearth of the type of realistic characters I am concerned with in this paper. Even Brown in the attempt to circumvent this problem takes recourse in a circular argument which moves between the question of choice and no choice and settles on none.

Flora Nwapa's first two novels, Efuru (1966) and Idu (1966) are the best known. They both provide a concentrated treatment of the usual themes of African women writers--marriage, polygamy, motherhood or barrenness; abuse or desertions by an irresponsible husband; the circumscription of the woman's life by the community and the ultimate moment of decision whether to stay in or leave the marriage. Early critics have commented on the difficulty of analysing Nwapa's heroines and their predicament because she encloses them within a perfected mould. Efuru and Idu are beautiful, generous to a fault, forgiving to erring husbands and abusive neighbours; enterprising and economically independent, the last two being factors which the student of African culture can easily identify with as long-standing historical facts and cultural practice. Margaret Laurence speaks for many critics when she writes about Efuru:

> She chooses men who are well aware of her beauty and capabilities but who are far from being in themselves strong characters. She is an excellent wife-loving, patient, good-humoured, hard-working. She can even cook well. In a sense she nearly kills her husbands with kindness. She never points out her own qualities, and in fact seems almost unaware of them, so she cannot even be accused of being self-righteous. If she had been stupid or malicious, even occasionally, her men might have found her easier to live with.[10]

These comments go straight to the fundamental problem of communication in the work. Efuru is daring enough to defy social norms and traditional expectations; to marry Adizua and move into his house without the traditional dowry and parental consent. The gossips of the farmers, the market-

---

[10] Margaret Laurence. Long Drums and Cannons. London, Melbourne, Toronto: Macmillan, 1968, p. 189.

women, relatives and friends and neighbours pass her by as she weathers the loneliness and anguish of a seemingly delayed pregnancy. A child is finally born and later dies. She is deserted by a first husband, Adizua, whom she literally made, economically, and then by a second, Eneberi. Yet she remains painstaking and submits herself to the series of ceremonies and conventions of the community as they relate to motherhood and wifehood, while managing to defy those formulations which seem irrelevant and too restrictive to her own integrity as a woman. She is presented as a perfect combination of conformity, rebelliousness and positive individualism. She has clearly demonstrated her independence against the encroachment of the community. Brown strangely calls her story "one of growth" but growth into what? I call it one of escape, for after a cyclical journey from innocence to experience and marriage, the heroine not only seeks refuge in the worship of Uhamiri, the Woman of the Lake, but goes right back to her father's house. But Brown says the emphasis is "not on specific roles, but on the woman's need for a free choice of roles" in further support of his claim that individualism is a Western characteristic, in which case the African heroine can find happiness and self-fulfilment only if she defines her identity within a role also acceptable by the society. Naana Banyiwa-Horne misses this basic point when she celebrates Efuru's final choice as one which escapes the traditional prescriptions of the identity of women. Maryse Conde, whom Banyiwa-Horne dismisses is more sensitive to the escapist or fatalistic solution of the text which creates a sense of wasted talents, physical and mental endowments. Whether or not Uhamiri is the spiritual embodiment of her own identity or not Conde's statement that no happiness can be achieved for a woman except in childbearing does have some validity. She complains that

> ...Efuru for all her qualities and gifts considers her life as valueless since she fails to have a child. She can deliberately and wilfully decide to leave her husband and therefore live by herself but she cannot follow the logical consequences. She cannot find in herself enough resources to counterbalance her sterility and never thinks of devoting her energies to something else.[11]

[11] Naana Banyiwa-Horne. "African Womanhood: The contrasting perspectives of Flora Nwapa's Efuru and Elechi Amadi's The Concubine" Ngambika, Trenton, New Jersey: Africa WorldPress, 1986, p. 128.

In comparing Efuru to Ihuoma of The Concubine by Elechi Amadi, a central point which Feminist critics like Banyiwa Home should not ignore, is that in The Concubine for the first time in African literature, a man, Ekwueme, chooses to dare a god and die on behalf of a woman he loves; and that the male characters suffer more in the hands of the sea-god than Ihuoma does.

Idu is similar to Efuru in its thematic concerns, marriage, motherhood, community versus the individual; and as usual the community prevails and Idu abandons the child she wanted so much and wills herself to death after the death of her husband; romantic, escapist, irresponsible, selfish? The reader is abandoned in an artistic quagmire and is being compelled to accept a heroine who shrinks into death rather than confront her problems. Once more a positive, strong enterprising heroine is not allowed to grow. Nwapa allows a suffocating faceless community system to strangle her, rather than allow her to work out her own individuality however rigorous and painful the process. Here social and artistic realism have been blatantly violated.

In her short stories Nwapa follows her female characters into the impersonal and exploitative environment of the city, Lagos, where they are victimised, abused and exploited within and without the family, but with the short novel, One is Enough, she switches over to the woman who confronts her own suffering in a childless marriage and seeks fame and fulfilment outside, but with her yearning for children fulfilled. But Amaka's choice of a Catholic priest for the father of her twin boys is the extreme of the former tradition-bound heroines. The former domesticated Amaka, wife of Obiora, succumbs totally to the corrupting influence of the city. This time the city prevails, never the woman.

Buchi Emecheta is another voice which champions the cause of African women even more directly than Nwapa, and certainly more intensively. She parades similar themes: the dowry, childless marriages, the non-male child marriage and what Brown calls "an intense confrontation with a male oriented world" which consistently violates the woman's sense of herself as a useful and fulfilled human being. From childhood to adulthood her needs and feelings are marginalised, first by father, next by husband and finally even by her children. The central metaphor is woman as slave, and in The Slave Girl (1977) she explores this theme in its literalness as a set of slave girls, Ojebeta and her mates, are physically, economically and sexually exploited by a rich slave-owning household. After such continuous degradation freedom finally comes for Ojebeta, but surprisingly she opts for a change of master by marrying Jacob, another form of slavery; so used is she to slavery that she prefers it to freedom. In the Ditch (1972) and Second Class Citizen (1974) are autobiographical and in both, the heroine, Ada, who is the author, suffers discrimination in Britain and the humiliation of living on the Dole. In the second novel, she grows and transcends the abuses of a cruel and insensitive husband, an unsuccessful marriage, recovers her sense of self worth and mends her battered identity. But in the rest of her novels, women are victims of their families, their husbands and their own internalised sense of worthlessness. She says of Ojebeta:

> Ojebeta was content and did not want more of life; she was happy in her husband, happy to be submissive, even to accept an occasional beating because that was what she had been brought up to believe a wife should expect.[12]

This is a good illustration of a female writer unconsciously accepting a female stereotype, the eternal subordinate and happy slave stereotype. As easy as it is for a history of long subordination to totally kill the spirit even the consciousness of freedom, to accord the phenomenon a permanent application and ignore the basic yearning for freedom in most human beings, simply converts the exception to the rule.

In The Bride Price (1976) the young adolescent heroine demonstrates resiliency, intelligence, sensitivity and early maturity through suffering; all these qualities and her rebellion against the social ostracization of the "Osu" predictably come to nothing, because of a brooding sense of fate--the same fate of a socially and historically defined destiny from which the novelist never allows her women characters to escape. She sacrifices Akunna and her young husband to the ancient curse which prescribes death for any bride whose bride price is not paid. The slave mentality runs in most of Emecheta's heroines: Akunna, Ojebeta and Nnu Ego with her monumental suffering. Her works lack

---

[12] Buchi Emecheta. The Slave Girl. United Kingdom: Fontana/Collins, 1977, p. 184.

positive images of women; rather they exhibit apathy, remain stupidly long-suffering without the aspiration to freedom or possibility of transcendence. Nnu Ego lives and dies as a slave of her society, her husband and her children; the only recognition she gets is an impressive funeral, one which symbolically re-enacts the story of a slave girl's death and rebirth, and a dominant motif in the novel.

Brown was right when he wrote that Emecheta's rhetoric of protest often betrays symptoms of an uncritical response to Western modes of perceiving and describing Africans; that Africans often appear as "natives" in her works, and that there are often the familiar Western contrasts between civilization on the one hand, and Nigerian "superstitions" or crudeness on the other. Her themes, characters and their responses to conflicts, and the resolution of their plots amply demonstrate this claim. Her attitude is condescending, static, unrealistic and ultimately fatalistic. This explains why in the nineteen eighties, with millions of Nigerian female graduates in universities, university teaching and other forms of university service; in industry and self-employment, politics and national service, the author posits the cultural assimilation of a female graduate as a serious problem. In Double Yoke, Nko's undergraduate boyfriend, Ete Kamba, in spite of his own education, feels threatened by her so-called independence and self-assertiveness which live in words rather than actions. Their love affair does not however prevent the heroine from succumbing to a strange sexual relationship with Rev. Professor Ikot in order to obtain a first-class degree. Her problem is lack of self-confidence; or is it inordinate ambition? She relies on her sexuality rather than merit or individual ability. Through it all she remains passive and confused, undercutting her previous avowal of feminism before Ete Kamba. The conflict remains superficially ideological throughout. The heroine eventually becomes pregnant by the Professor and courageously decides to keep her baby and return to school at a later date. But such a sign of growth has no place in Emecheta's literary world, so she claps her fated machine on the heroine; the father dies at that difficult stage of her life, forcing her back on Ete Kamba who has no respect for her. Emecheta sees the woman as the eternal weakling and masochistic victim.

Has this attitude been dislodged in Destination Biafra (1982) her latest novel? Debbie Ogedemgbe, the heroine, is the clear incarnation of Emecheta's political convictions about women and marriage. But from Nko to Debbie, she moves from personal to political themes, from personal career and marriage, to sex and war. The book deals with the Nigerian Civil War, which the author calls a masculine theme. Debbie, an Oxford graduate is sent literally to seduce Abosi, the rebel leader, and a former boyfriend into submission. She is an unabashed feminist, Europeanised and loud; and this leads to her sexual victimization by both the Nigerian and Biafran soldiers. Significantly, like the author, she wants to be a writer, and at the end, she mouths her feminist anti-imperialist ideology when she repudiates her former British boyfriend, Alan Gray as a gesture of her African authenticity. In spite of this feminist posture she remains shallow, predictable, static; her prouncements contrived and simplistic. She is a flat character and does not develop. As is usual in Emecheta's works, she finds fulfilment only outside marriage.

The critic of Emecheta's works is confronted with the problem of evaluative criteria, in assessing the writer's commitment to social, political, sexual and human reality. Women writers must face the issue of literary ethics, taking into account the enlightenment of their readership. It is part of the moral function which these writers embrace. In exploiting Gray, Debbie undermines her own humanity, unlike characters in Bessie Head's novels.

With Head's novels we attain the end of the search for the authentic voice for African women in literature. In her novels, themes and style attain balance and maturity. She expands gender issues, sex, oppression, racial identity to universal heights. No writer, male or female, perhaps anywhere in the world can claim a deeper experience or understanding of loneliness than Head; with a son as the only relation she knew in this vast universe; yet the pain, anger, fear are channelled into a literary style whose hallmark is maturity. She is concerned with the issues of power, identity and uprootedness for both men and women. She uses her own life as a paradigm for the abuse, rejection and exploitation of women in society but her bleak social and moral landscape are artistically balanced with almost a fiery optimism in the ability of people to influence their own destiny. Her women characters, Margaret Cadmore, Elizabeth, Paulina Sebeso, even the super powerless Thako are offered the possibility of growth and transcendence. Head's books are not named after female characters but the women do move the world in which they live and do authenticate their humanity.

In Maru (1971), Margaret Cadmore is totally alone--she is fatherless and motherless, born in an asylum, raised by a foster parent, abused by fellow children in school, avoided by teacher colleagues, but her quiet presence raises a storm in a traditional community, and among royalty. Even while being victimized, she asserts herself and identity both through her intelligence, beauty, resilience and artistic creations. Despite the permanent pain of being torn away ruthlessly from her first love, she finds happiness and self-fulfilment somehow.

Elizabeth in A Question of Power (1974), finds love from unexpected sources but mainly peace after the horrors and torments she undergoes in the novel. These horrors arose from her feelings of racial and sexual inadequacies.

In the cooperatives, Paulina Sebeso, Mma Milipede and Maria also grow into self-realization after periods of suffering, loneliness and abuse. This evolutionary imperative does not prevent Head from criticising women both in and out of marriage for often acquiescing in their own abuse and subjugation. In her short stories she explores various types of marriages, and sexual relationships; but when the victims one day turn husband-murderers, as four of her female characters do, Head understands; so do we.

Finally the problem of private growth as a prerequisite for social change must be confronted by African women writers. They must be willing to embrace some of Head's tough-minded realism and steer away from unnecessary sentimentalism and fatalism. Women have always been victims, at all times and in all places, but there are also, especially in Africa, abundant demonstration of an admirable refusal to accept the permanent restrictiveness of society; a dogged determination to redefine their own lives and needs, sometimes with success, other times with failure. But these attempts must be acknowledged in a literary tradition which claims to be humanistic and only when African women writers also grow as their characters do, in sincerity, in sensitivity, subtlety and breadth of vision, like Bessie Head, can we truly begin to celebrate the emergence of authentic female voices in African literature.